CUMBRIA'S INDUSTRIAL PAST
through the lens of Mike Davies-Shiel

Published by

Cumbria Industrial History Society

Published by Cumbria Industrial History Society

www.cumbria-industries.org.uk

Copyright © Cumbria Industrial History Society

First published 2017

Typeset in Garamond

ISBN 978 1 9997049 0 2

All rights reserved, no part of this publication may be reproduced, stored in a retrieval system or transmitted, in any form or by any means, electronic, mechanical, photocopying or otherwise, without prior permission in writing from the Cumbria Industrial History Society

Typeset and printed by MTP Media Ltd

Front cover: Backbarrow Blue Works from the Iron Works site

CONTENTS

Preface i

Map iii

Chapter 1. Mining and Quarrying 1
- Introduction
- Langdale Axe Factories
- Slate
- Barytes & Zinc
- Copper & Lead
- Coal
- Lime
- Peat

Chapter 2. Iron and Steel 21
- Introduction
- Hodbarrow Mines
- Backbarrow Iron Works
- Iron and Steel Making at Moss Bay, Workington
- Foundries

Chapter 3. Water Power 57

Chapter 4. Corn Milling & Brewing 61

Chapter 5. Snuff 71

Chapter 6. Woodland and Associated Industries 75
- Coppicing
- Uses of Coppice Wood
- Basket-Making
- Clog-Making
- Bobbin Mills and Wood Turning
- Brushes
- Tanning
- Charcoal

Chapter 7. Textiles 93
- Wool
- Flax & Linen
- Cotton

Chapter 8. Backbarrow Blue Works 107

Chapter 9. Transport 111
- Roads
- Railways
- Water Transport
- Air Transport

Index 123

Reproduced by kind permission of The Mail, Barrow

PREFACE

Mike Davies-Shiel

This book was born of Cumbria Industrial History Society's wish to celebrate the life's work of Mike Davies-Shiel (1929-2009) in the investigation and interpretation of Cumbria's industrial past, and to share it with a wider audience.

Mike was a schoolmaster by profession, working in Windermere Grammar School and the Lakes School until his early retirement in 1986. The fieldwork that was an integral part of his subject specialisms – geography and geology – quickly led to him developing a passionate interest in the then neglected area of local industrial history. He was a founder member of the Cumbria Industrial History Society and, latterly, its President.

From the late 1950s, until his death in 2009, he travelled widely in Cumbria, seeking out former industrial sites and documenting whatever he found, always combining his fieldwork with complementary archival research. As well as recording the field evidence left by defunct industries, he visited those still active, but either threatened, or in steep decline, paying particular attention to the knowledge and experience of the men and women still at work.

He was especially interested in the techniques of traditional woodland management, notably coppicing and charcoal burning, watermills, and the textile and early iron industries. He was permitted to go underground at Hodbarrow iron mine just before it closed, helped organise the excavation of Stony Hazel forge, and became the chronicler of the Backbarrow Iron Works during its final few years, and of the Blue Works 20 years later.

During the whole of this time, he carried a camera and it is from his vast collection of slides and negatives, the fruit of half a century of close observation, that the photographs in this book have been selected.

The Mike Davies-Shiel Collection

It was always Mike's intention that all his papers and photographic slides and negatives should be left to the Cumbria Archive Service. However, when the CIHS suggested that the photographs might be digitised and thus made much more widely available for researchers, he readily agreed, and with the support of his wife, Noree, the copyright was given to the society after his death.

The photographic collection consists of over 20,000 slides and negatives, of which some 18,000 have been digitised. They were housed in themed slide boxes, of various sizes, and the first task for the Society was to give each slide or negative a unique reference number. For example, the first picture in Chapter 1, 34-26, is the 26th slide in Box 34, 'Cumbria's Minerals'. The caption underneath the picture, in italics, is based on Mike's notes on the margins of the slide.

The numbering of each slide and the transfer of reference numbers and Mike's comments onto record sheets was done by a small team of volunteers, to whom the society extends its sincere gratitude; without them the project could not have proceeded. The information was then entered on a database.

The original slides, after being digitally copied, have been transferred to the Carlisle Archive Centre for safe storage. The database, with thumb-nail copies of the images, has been uploaded to the Cumbria Archive Service catalogue – CASCAT. For further information about searching CASCAT and purchasing copies of the images please see the society's website www.cumbria-industries.org.uk

The professional digital copying of the images was made possible by grants and donations from the following organisations and individuals, to whom we are most grateful:

CWAAS Research Committee
Cumbria Community Foundation
The Hadfield Trust
Curwen Archive Trust
Kirby Archive Trust
Sir John Fisher Foundation
Gilbert Gilkes & Gordon Ltd
Cartmel Fell & District Local History Society
Duddon Valley Local History Group
Sir James Cropper
Oliver Barratt

buildings were demolished or converted into housing, and tourism became the prime industry of Cumbria.

The text has been written by various members of the CIHS and seeks to place each photo in its historical context; particular thanks are given to Helen Caldwell and Graham Brooks in this regard. The society would like to acknowledge Noree Davies-Shiel's help and encouragement, and Mark Brennand's assiduous proof-reading and valuable suggestions. Any errors are solely attributable to the society.

Geoff Brambles, Chairman CIHS

June 2017

About the Book

This book is intended to highlight some of Mike's most interesting photographs, illustrating a range of industries that had once flourished in Cumbria and some which were still active at the time. All the photographs are taken from the Mike Davies-Shiel collection and are believed to have been taken by him between the late 1950s and 2006.

This period saw a lot of change. Ownership of manufacturing became increasingly globalised and concentrated in the hands of fewer, larger companies. Cheap imports undermined the profitability of small firms, and synthetic fibres successfully competed with woollens. Some older works closed because they were unable to meet modern standards of health and safety for workers and environmental protection.

Mike managed to photograph the final days of many of these industries before the

CUMBRIA

Places Referred To In The Book

195-17 Elterwater Slate. June 1966

MINING AND QUARRYING

Due to its very varied geology, Cumbria has probably had a greater range of minerals and rocks extracted from it over the centuries than any other county in Britain. This history of extraction dates back to the Neolithic stone axe factories of the central Lakeland fells. There was probably copper mining in the Bronze Age, although direct evidence is lacking and may well have been removed by later mining activity. The Romans certainly quarried stone for their buildings and especially Hadrian's Wall, as well as mining for lead and copper. The mining of lead and copper continued during the medieval period, but had a boost during Elizabethan times, with the arrival of German and Austrian miners. They brought new techniques to both mining and the processing of ores including the introduction of rail systems for the movement of ore and rock, and developed the valuable wad (graphite) mines in Borrowdale, which led to the development of the pencil industry in Keswick.

The late eighteenth and nineteenth centuries saw the major development of the mineral mines in the Lake District and in the Pennines. A large number of mines opened or expanded in this period. Some, such as Coniston Copper mines, became very successful and continued in production into the twentieth century, but others had poor veins and were never a commercial success. As industry developed, minerals and metals which once were considered of little value such as zinc and barytes found a commercial use, and some mines such as Potts Gill and Nenthead were reworked, thus extending their life.

From the 17th century, through to the closure of Whitehaven's Haig Pit in 1986 with the loss of 800 jobs, coal mining was a major industry in West Cumbria, with smaller deposits being worked in other parts of the county.

Substantial investment by local families, particularly the Lowthers in Whitehaven, led to innovation in mining techniques, the building of harbours for the export of coal, and town development with distinctive Georgian architectural styles.

Most of the local stones have been exploited for building, especially the limestones in the south of the county and the sandstones on the west coast and in the Eden valley. The colours and shapes of the various local building stones determine much of the character of the towns, villages and drystone walls of the county.

34-26 Fault vein. Copper mine, Wetherlam, Coniston. March 1975

34-26. The line of surface workings marks the position of a copper-bearing vein that was deposited along a geological fault.

Langdale Axe Factories

99-16 Stone axe quarry sites - Pike o'Stickle. February 2002

High up on the Langdale Pikes and continuing round to Glaramara and Scafell Pike there is exposed a layer of very hard, very fine-grained volcanic tuff, seen in **99-16** as the pale-coloured scree. Sometime during prehistory this resource was discovered, and by the Neolithic period, about 6,000 years ago, the stone was quarried extensively to manufacture polished stone axe blades.

On site, the rock was worked into pieces of suitable size and shape for axe-heads as shown in **99-30**. These rough-outs were then brought down to settlement sites, such as the one found at Ehenside Tarn, Beckermet, and painstakingly polished to an overall smooth finish. Tests have shown that to polish the cutting edge increases efficiency, but to polish the whole axe blade transformed its appearance into an item of aesthetic beauty. Once polished, the axe blades became important objects in their own right, and were traded over long distances.

99-30 Stone axe rough-outs; most are stained with manganese dioxide. December 1963

The main phase of archaeological exploration of the quarry workings began in the 1940s, but continued for many years. Mike participated in the early 1960s and **99-30** shows typical rough-outs and rejects found during one of his visits.

Slate

Lake District slate has been worked at least since the late thirteenth century, but the discovery of roofing slates in Ambleside fort and in the vicus of Maryport fort strongly suggest that there was slate quarrying at least as far back as the Roman period.

Cumbrian roofing slate was marketed widely, both at home and abroad, reaching a peak during the late nineteenth century. Despite its enviable reputation for durability, the competition from cheaper clay tiles and imported slate brought about a near-terminal decline in the Cumbrian slate industry during the latter part of the 20th century.

Two factors have ensured its survival. The first is diversification. As well as roofing slate, a wide range of other products have been developed, such as wall cladding, floor tiles, table tops and fire surrounds. Secondly, the Cumbrian industry has largely come under the ownership of a single company, Burlington Stone Co Ltd, which can more effectively control output and secure markets.

195-62 Sledge tracks on the Patterdale flank of Caudale Moor. October 1997

195-62. The earliest way of speeding up the transport of slates from high level riving sheds down to lower ground was by the use of wooden sledges. Operated by only one man, who controlled the descent by muscle power alone, and with the whole load behind him, this was a hazardous occupation, requiring great skill. The skids of the sledges quickly wore away the soil, producing well-marked grooves in the ground. These examples, immediately to the right of the valley shadow, can be seen zig-zagging through the bracken.

195-43 Honister slate quarries. 1964

195-43. The diagonal scar on the fellside marks the external incline on Honister Crags, once used to lower clogs of slate from the mine to the dressing sheds on the Hause. It was built in the 1880s to replace the sled tracks used to take the slates from the quarry to the Buttermere road. The incline was self-acting and consisted of a steeply inclined railway at a constant gradient, which required the construction of numerous slate embankments and cuttings through the rock face. A drum house at the top controlled the rate of descent of the full trucks and the rise of the empty ones. The route is now used as a tourist attraction, with a 'via ferrata' constructed along it.

195-48 Old slate workings, Coniston. February 1964

195-48. Due to the steepness of the mountainside on which the Coniston quarries were situated, rail transport was not suitable; overhead ropeways provided the answer. The original ropeway carried finished slates from Spion Kop quarry, just below the summit of the Old Man, to the road to allow onward transport. Further ropeways were added to allow clogs of slate to be brought from the various quarries to the processing sheds. Some of the derelict pylons still remain.

195-15 Flooded quarry, Elterwater. June 1966

195-15. Good quality slate was pursued downwards from ground level until the cost of pumping and the technical difficulties of raising the clogs of slate rendered further exploitation uneconomic. This quarry, however, has more recently been drained and re-worked.

195-2 shows the traditional technique of splitting a block of slate manually, using a hammer and chisel to divide it into two pieces of equal thickness.

195-2 A slate river at work, Elterwater. June 1966

6

195-3 Mechanical slate trimmer. Elterwater sheds. June 1966

195-8 A machine-sawn block of slate being manoeuvred by overhead crane, Elterwater. June 1966

195-3 and **195-8**. Mechanisation came to the slate industry with the machine cutting of the roughly hewn clogs of rock. Today the slate can be machined with great accuracy by computer controlled equipment to meet the precise requirements of architects, builders and artists. Much more efficient and versatile use is made of the raw material with a consequent dramatic reduction of waste. These photos show the casual attitude to health and safety at work 50 years ago.

195-67 Youngsters at risk – rock falls in slate quarry, Borrowdale. 1980

Barytes and Zinc

93-338 Road into the Force Crag Mine. July 1989

93-338. Force Crag Mine, at the head of Coledale, worked from 1820 - 1993. Lead, zinc and barytes (barium sulphate) were commercially extracted. The barium sulphate had medical uses, its high density making it opaque to X-rays, and was also used in paints, oil well-drilling lubricants and as a filler in paper-making.

93-346. The mine operated through nine levels. Externally the mine can be split into the lower and upper parts. Levels 0, 1, 2 and 3 served the lower part of the mine from c.1870. Levels 4 to 9 are in the upper part of the mine. In 1940 the two parts of the mine were connected by an aerial ropeway. In the 1950s Laporte Chemicals Ltd drove an internal incline between the lower and upper levels.

93-336 Fusing the explosive at Force Crag, No.1 adit portal. The explosive used was amatol – a mixture of TNT and ammonium nitrate.

93-340 shows one of the pylons that carried the aerial ropeway which allowed ore from the upper workings to be taken down the steep mountainside to the processing buildings in the valley bottom. Built in 1941 by Tampimex Oil Products Ltd, it was originally envisaged that it would carry the ore to a processing plant at Braithwaite, but it was changed to a direct descent to the processing plant in the valley. The ropeway

93-340 View from the upper workings looking N.E. down Coledale towards Braithwaite. June 1962

was, however, susceptible to the severe winter weather conditions of the Lake District. After years of disuse, the pylons were removed in 1972.

The National Trust now conserves the site and the processing mill is open occasionally for escorted visits.

93-346 No. 1 level's portal with engine shed. July 1989

Copper and Lead

*34-11 Goldscope Mine, Vale of Newlands, November 1984.
The name derives from the German Gotes gab – God's gift.*

34-11. The first written record of Goldscope mine dates back to the early 13th century, though surface working had probably been carried on for many years before that, possibly in pre-Roman times.

It mainly produced chalcopyrite, a copper ore, though some lead (galena) was also found. In 1564 the German miners drove the adit, without the use of explosives, to exploit the substantial copper deposit, and before the end of the century they installed an internal waterwheel to raise the ore and drain the workings. The mine appears to have been worked intermittently until 1852 when, in pursuit of the dwindling copper vein, the copper adit intersected a substantial lead vein, leading to a period of great prosperity which was to last 12 years. Five thousand tons of lead ore, yielding 22,000 ounces of silver, were produced before the mine closed in 1864, the 40 foot waterwheel having proved inadequate for the prevention of flooding at greater depths.

93-514. Roughton Gill has a long history of lead and copper mining going back to the Elizabethans, if not earlier. The picture shows what is probably the best example of a hush in the Lake District. Hushes were a means of searching for veins. Dams were built to collect water upslope of the area to be prospected. Water was then released to flow down the hillside, scouring away soil and other surface deposits to expose the underlying rock and, with luck, a mineral vein. Once a vein had been exposed and worked, further hushing could carry away waste rock to clean up the vein for further working. If the vein was not suitable for open working, then levels were driven into the vein to work the mineral, as occurred here. The use of hushes was eventually banned due to the pollution it caused in local watercourses. The mine worked from 1790 to 1880.

93-514 The Roughton Gill hushes, Caldbeck Fells. March 1989.

93-109. Greenside was the largest lead mine in Lakeland. There appears to have been some working in the mid 18th century, but the main workings commenced in 1820 and continued until 1962 by which time all commercial ore had been removed. The mine consisted of a single vein running north – south and worked over a length of two miles and to a depth of 3,000 ft.

A smelt mill and de-silvering works (galena, the principal lead ore, contains a small percentage of silver, usually commercially worth removing for sale) were built on site in the 1830s, with a long flue up the fell behind to remove the toxic fumes from the working area. It also allowed lead fumes to condense, coating the flue lining with a deposit that could be later recovered and reprocessed.

93-109 Greenside lead mine tips, Patterdale. 1968.

In 1891 the mine was the first to install electric haulage with a winding engine on the Smith's shaft. The electricity was generated by a turbine driven by water from Keppel Cove. This also allowed electric locomotives to be introduced in 1893 on the Lucy Level, another first for the UK.

Towards the end of the mine's life the Atomic Weapons Research Establishment detonated two large charges of TNT deep underground, monitoring the shock waves on seismographs in various locations from Patterdale to Sedbergh. Operation Orpheus, as it was called, showed that in some circumstances underground explosions could be attenuated so that they were not detected and this information led to the collapse of the nuclear test ban negotiations with Russia in 1961.

93-185. Although copper and lead mines did not generally have problems with methane gas, in 1952 a fire in the woodwork deep inside Greenside mine caused the death of 4 men, who were overcome by carbon monoxide. A Mines Rescue Team was set up, with a canary, following this accident. Canaries were widely used to detect harmful gases such as methane and carbon monoxide in underground workings. The birds would show signs of distress before the miners were affected, thus allowing safe evacuation of the area. It was not until 1987 that canaries were replaced by hand-held gas detectors in all British coal mines.

93-260. Myers Head mine consisted of two parts: three levels and a shaft on the ridge leading to Hartsop Dodd and a shaft at the junction of Pasture Beck and Hayeswater Gill, which is the part shown in this photo. The shaft was sunk by the Low Hartsop Mining Company in 1867-1868 to reach the vein at a depth of 55 metres. A 30 ft diameter waterwheel was installed to drive the pumps to de-water the shaft. Water was

93-185 Rescue worker, Arnold Lewis, and his "yaller belly", Greenside lead mine. March 1962

drawn from Hayeswater Gill near the point where the leat for the local corn mill came off. The water for the wheel was conveyed by an iron launder, supplied by Cowans Sheldon of Carlisle, carried on the dry stone pillars which remain, although several of the northern launder supports were destroyed by the severe storm and flooding in December 2015. The mine was not very productive; it closed in 1878 after just 12 years, due to a disastrous underground flood from which the miners were lucky to escape alive.

93-260 Myers Head lead mine near Hartsop, showing waterwheel pit and headrace supports. The mine entrance is near the large tree. 1983.

The upper Nent valley was one of the major lead mining areas in the North Pennines. A smelt mill was built there in 1736 by Colonel George Liddle, who had obtained a number of mine leases in the area from the Commissioners of Greenwich Hospital, who had been granted the rights after the execution of the 3rd Earl of Derwentwater for the part he played in the Jacobite uprising of 1715. The leases were taken over by the London Lead Company in 1745. They expanded the mining operations in the area and developed the smelt mill to process the increased ore production.

93-379. Many of the London Lead Company shareholders were Quakers who put the welfare of their workforce high on their list of priorities, leading to the development of the village of Nenthead. They were also keen to use the latest developments in their mines and smelt mills to improve efficiency.

93-379 Nenthead village with the lead company's reading room and fountain. 1970

93-373. This large wheel pit was for the Stagg condenser. Joseph Dickinson Stagg was the manager of the mills and washing floors at Nenthead lead mine. In 1843 he patented a fume condenser to decrease the amount of 'fume' (small particles of lead dust etc that are lost up the chimney during smelting). The wheel provided the power to air pumps which drew the fumes from the smelting hearths through a series of water-filled cisterns. The large wall carried the bob beam which transferred the power from the wheel to the pumps.

The London Lead Company controlled the leases until 1882, when they were taken over by the Nenthead and Tynedale Lead and Zinc Company. They operated till 1896 when the Belgian Vielle Montagne Zinc Company took over the leases and operated the mines in the area until 1949. Mining at Nenthead ceased in 1961.

93-373 Nenthead 45 ft waterwheel pit. June 1989.

Coal

7-45 Saltom, built 1731, & Haig Pits, Whitehaven. Note collapsed cliffs. July 1967

7-57 Haig Pit, Whitehaven. July 1967

7-45 shows the old and new of undersea coal working. At the base of the cliff are remains of Saltom pit, sunk between March 1730 and February 1732, initially to a depth of 480ft. It was the introduction of Newcomen engine pumps to the area that allowed this pit not only to mine coal from under the sea, but also to take water which drained from other inland pits. The original shaft was oval with a wooden partition down the centre; one side was used for pumping whilst coals were drawn up the other side by a horse engine (gin). Initially the coals were to be exported from a small harbour built next to the pit. This was unsuccessful and a drift was driven into the cliff to connect up with Ravenhill pit on the cliff above, allowing the coals to be hauled up to the cliff top.

The Saltom site is under threat both from the sea and also from cliff erosion.

7-57. On the cliff top is Haig Pit with its buildings and railway sidings. Two shafts were sunk between 1914 and 1918. The pit, along with the rest of the Whitehaven colliery, was worked by a number of companies with varying success until nationalisation in 1947. The pit continued working until 1986 by which time they had mined coal from under the Irish Sea to a distance of over 4 miles.

The Haig Pit site is preserved with the steam winding engines still in situ, operated by compressed air.

7-159. The sinking of Jane Pit was started in 1843 to try and revitalise the failing coal trade in Workington after the sea had broken into Chapel Bank Colliery on 30th July 1837, leading to the death of 27 miners. The sinking was seriously hampered by both water and gas. They reached the Hamilton seam in 1846 (73 fathoms). Low production, excessive water and a lack of funds for investment led eventually to the closure of the pit in 1893. The remains today are the castellated engine house and chimney.

7-159 Jane Pit Workington.

Lime

149-80 Old lime kiln, near Scales, Low Furness. Stepped arch. May 1989

Limestone is widespread in Cumbria and has been exploited at least since Roman times. Limestone is chemically calcium carbonate, if this is heated to over 900°C a chemical reaction occurs, driving off carbon dioxide to leave calcium oxide, commonly called quicklime. This has a number of uses including fertilizer and for making whitewash and lime mortar for building.

The quicklime, calcium oxide, if exposed to water, reacts and becomes calcium hydroxide (slaked lime). This reaction is strongly exothermic (produces heat), and occasionally a wooden cart loaded with quicklime would be set alight if caught in a shower of rain. Slaked lime will absorb carbon dioxide in the air to give calcium carbonate again. This is the chemical basis for lime mortar.

149-80. A typical small field kiln, probably dating from the late 18th or early 19th century. Lime was applied to "sweeten" existing pastures and was a particularly important component of the process of enclosure and improvement of previously uncultivated land, by helping to release soil nutrients. The kiln would be filled with alternating layers of coal and limestone, burnt, then emptied. These cycles would be repeated until sufficient lime was obtained for use locally.

Commercial kilns near Bothel are shown in **149-177** and **149-180**. These are bigger, more modern, versions of the small field kiln (**149-80**). The left hand pot is full, with the top layer of limestone showing. The right hand pot is partially empty, revealing the slagged firebrick lining. Large kilns such as these can be kept burning continuously, burnt lime being removed at the bottom, causing the fire to descend in the kiln and allowing more fuel and limestone to be added at the top.

149-177 Lime kiln tops, Bothel, Wigton. 3m x 6m at top. June 1970

149-180. The layer of coal below the top layer of limestone is just starting to burn, showing that the fire has reached the top of the kiln and burnt lime can be drawn from the bottom to lower the fire and allow the kiln to be refilled.

149-180 Burning kiln. June 1970

34-49. These modern steel, gas fired lime kilns next to the M6 at Shap were built to produce lime for use as a flux in the steel industry. Originally the limestone was quarried from Hardendale Nab; it is now brought by road from a quarry at Wilson Scar to the north of the village. The burnt lime is transported from the site by rail. The Ravenscraig steel works in Scotland mentioned in the caption are long closed, but in 2017 the plant is still providing lime for other parts of the steel industry.

34-49 Lime kilns, Shap. Flux for Ravenscraig steel works. June 1976

Peat

Peat is formed where water levels are consistently too high, and oxygen levels too low to allow vegetation, especially Sphagnum moss, to decay fully. Lowland 'raised' bogs are concentrated around Morecambe Bay and the Solway, but peat may also be formed in upland 'blanket' bogs where rainfall is high and drainage limited. Both types may be identified on maps as a Moss.

Peat was used by smelting industries in Cumbria before the railways made coal accessible to most areas. The iron furnace at Lowwood, Haverthwaite (1748-1785), for instance, used large quantities of peat from the local mosses, although the iron thus produced was inferior to that of the nearby Backbarrow iron furnace, which used charcoal. In those areas where it was easily extracted, and coal and other forms of fuel were not readily available, peat was used as a fuel for industries requiring heat, such as in limekilns and corn drying kilns. Peat was also used for household heating and cooking purposes. Rights of turbary allowed householders to cut peat from a specified plot for their own use. It was also transported into towns such as Carlisle for both commercial and domestic use, until coal became cheaper with the coming of the railways. More recently, peat has been extracted on a large scale for horticultural use, often using purpose built machinery.

149-51. Cecil Walling cutting peat on Middle Foulshaw Moss. May 1990.

The traditional techniques of peat cutting, barrowing and drying are illustrated in **149-51**, **149-48** and **149-34**. Cecil Walling is seen using a cutting tool with a flange on one side to produce peats of a consistent size and his brother Larry carries the peats on a traditional peat barrow to the drying area, where they are stacked and left to dry.

149-48 Larry Walling with peat barrow at Foulshaw, Witherslack. May 1990.

149-34. Peats being stacked. Middle Foulshaw Moss, with Larry Walling. May 1990.

114-41 Peat Hut above Eskdale. September 1989.

Traditional peat digging was weather dependent and restricted to late spring and summer to allow enough time for the peats to dry out before winter. Once dry, the peats were carried to a storage barn or shed. This granite-built example (**114-41**) is particularly stout, but at Foulshaw Moss peats were also stored in a motley assortment of corrugated iron or wooden garden sheds as shown in **149-55**.

Peat cutting has virtually died out in Cumbria. Foulshaw Moss has been purchased by the Cumbria Wildlife Trust and peat extraction there has ceased.

149-55 1989's peat in shed, Foulshaw. May 1990.

IRON AND STEEL

Cumbria was fortunate in having good deposits of iron ore. These ranged from massive deposits of haematite in the limestones of south and west Cumbria to veins of haematite in some parts of the Lake District. Lower grade ores were also found in the Pennines. Direct evidence for early mining and processing of iron ore is absent from the county until the 13th century, when the monks of Furness Abbey were mining and processing ores. The mining of ores gradually increased as general mining techniques improved, and production peaked in the latter part of the 19th century.

123-7 Haematite kidney ore and specularite (black) in roof at Florence Mine, Egremont. September 1993

The early processing of ores was in a bloomery. This did not produce liquid iron, but a 'bloom', a semi-solid mass of iron that still had a large amount of slag in it. The original bloomeries used hand bellows to generate sufficient blast to raise the temperature inside the furnace, so the furnaces were small. Charcoal was the fuel and due to the quantity required, the bloomeries were generally built near to the supply of charcoal, with the iron ore carried to them. Over 300 bloomery sites have been identified in Cumbria.

Once a bloom had been produced in the furnace, it was taken out and hammered to remove the excess slag. The iron could then be reheated and forged into required implements.

Bloomery furnaces were often made of clay, and few have survived, but their sites can often be identified by the presence of slag. (**32-101**)

32-101 Bloomery slags, Angler's Crag, Ennerdale. September 1984

Further improvements led to the introduction of water power to work the bellows from about 1300, increasing the size of the bloom produced. These furnaces are classified as stringhearths. By the end of the 17th century water power was also being applied to the hammer to process the bloom. These combined water powered sites became housed in permanent buildings, and are known as bloomsmithies (**32-72**). The water powered bellows created higher temperatures in the furnace and this allowed some of the impurities in the ore to form a liquid slag that could be drawn off from the furnace. The quantity of iron now being produced was greater than local needs and it could be sold in other areas.

32-72 Langstrath bloomsmithy, Borrowdale

The ever increasing demand for iron led to the development of blast furnaces. These initially continued to use charcoal as fuel. The early furnaces were stone structures; the blast was at first produced using bellows powered by waterwheels, but steam engines later provided the power, and blowing engines were introduced instead of bellows. Eight blast furnaces were built in the Furness area between 1711 and 1748, the one at Backbarrow continuing to work until 1966.

The blast furnace produced cast iron, which had a high carbon content, making it brittle. Molten iron was run out of the furnace into sand beds to form ingots (the beds were said to look like baby pigs suckling the sow and so the iron was called pig iron), or directly into a mould. Cast iron could be converted into wrought iron by reducing its carbon content. This was achieved by reheating in a finery hearth with bellows, which both heated the iron, and allowed air to be passed across the surface, the oxygen in the air reacting with carbon to produce carbon dioxide. The bloom

6-155 Stony Hazel Forge, Rusland, anvil and hammer area. August 1969

was then hammered again to give wrought iron (**6-155 and 6-4**). Stony Hazel was one of a number of forges which took pig iron from Backbarrow and converted it to wrought iron. Mike and Dr John Marshall led the excavation of the site between 1968 and 1974.

88-336. The use of charcoal mostly tied the furnaces and forges to the Furness woodlands, but new technology allowed the use of coke, and from the 1840s new ironworks were built closer to the ore fields, at 21 Cumbrian locations including Ulverston, Barrow, Askam, Millom, Whitehaven, Workington and Maryport.

Cast iron had its uses for industry and in the home, and numerous small foundries were established in Cumbrian towns in the late 18th and 19th centuries.

The next major technological development was the mass production of steel. Steel has a carbon content between cast and wrought iron. The carbon content can be varied to give the steel different properties, as can the addition of other metals to give alloys.

6-4 Stony Hazel hammer head. August 1969

88-336 Barrow ironworks. November 1958

Early steel-making involved packing wrought iron bars and charcoal into crucibles and heating them in a chest for up to a week. This slow and small scale process was known as cementation.

The first big breakthrough was the development of the Bessemer converter in 1856. This allowed large quantities of cast iron to be converted to steel in a short period of time by blowing air through molten iron. Bessemer converters were installed at Workington in 1877.

The Bessemer process was superseded by the open-hearth furnace and then by the electric arc furnace, both of which were used in Cumbria.

Hodbarrow Mines

These mines near Millom, which raised 25m tons of some of the richest haematite iron ore in the world during 105 years of mining, were the last survivors of a Furness and South Cumberland industry which once spanned both sides of the Duddon Estuary.

The iron ore occurred as haematite, mainly as large, irregular flat-lying replacements of the Lower Carboniferous limestones of the area. These ore deposits in the Hodbarrow area were overlain by water-logged sand and gravels which caused significant problems for the mine throughout its life. The ores had a metallic iron content of about 60%.

Iron ore was being mined at the Hill of Millom in the late 1840s and attempts had been made at Hodbarrow, but without success, until in 1855 a lease was granted by the Second Earl of Lonsdale to Nathaniel Caine and John Barratt, who formed the Hodbarrow Mining Company. Serious work then started on the site at The Old Engine Shaft. Caine (1808 - 1877) was a partner in a Liverpool firm of iron merchants and John Barratt (1793 – 1866) was a miner from Cornwall who had worked at the Duke of Devonshire's lead mines at Grassington, and managed the Coniston copper mines from around 1830.

Barratt bought the Steel Green estate, which was advertised in 1855 as having potential as a sea bathing resort. A year later he had found an 80 ft (24 m) seam of solid haematite iron ore. He did not live long enough to see how the mine and the new town of Millom would develop.

In May 1864 Hodbarrow employed just 120 men; by December 1866 there were 265 working underground and by 1871 the workforce had grown to 482. The 1870s were the boom years at Hodbarrow. Profits grew from £47,000 in 1870/71 to £181,000 in 1873/74. In 1892 to 1893 Hodbarrow raised 538,979 tons of ore - 43 per cent of all the ore raised in Cumberland that year, with 1,000 men employed.

3-32 Annie Lowther Pit & Arnold Pit (red brick). June 1968

3-32. Annie Lowther pit was sunk in 1869. In 1878 a new 70 inch (1.78 m) pumping engine from the Perran Foundry in Cornwall was installed in the shaft to cope with the inrushes of water, sand and gravel. This pump was moved to No. 10 pit in 1910, where it could still be seen in 1968. The pit was eventually closed in 1924. The Millom ironworks are in the background.

3-5 Hodbarrow Mine. Main mine before flooding. March 1968

3-5 shows the broken ground of Hodbarrow mine subsidence in March 1968 before much of this area was allowed to fill with water. Because of the thickness of the seam of iron ore at over 100 ft (30 m) in places, it was mined by a technique called 'top-slicing', whereby slices of ore were taken at about 10 ft thickness on a pillar and stall method, working down through the ore body. The pillars and intervening floors were then removed. Because the ore was near the surface, the effect of removing the whole seam was to cause the overlying ground to subside drastically, giving a very uneven ground surface known locally as 'broken ground'. As mining progressed, this fractured ground surface started letting more surface water through into the mine and more pumping was required. The inner barrier started to collapse in 1909, after the limestone roof under the wall started to break up. By September 1910 parts had already slumped up to 26 ft (8 m). From 1922, mining techniques changed to 'bottom-slicing', the voids being deliberately filled with sand to reduce subsidence.

3-97 Typical roadway with sand pipe. Feb 1968

3-122 Hodbarrow Inner Barrier. Old Mine Pits Nos.5, Annie Lowther, 8, and 10. June 1968

3-122. This substantial Inner Barrier was built in 1888-90 from concrete, with stonework facing, and an inner core of puddled clay. The barrier was needed as the mine workings were progressing towards the foreshore and it became a worry that seawater could start entering the workings. The building of the barrier allowed access to between 4 and 5 million tons of iron ore. However, it proved no match for mine subsidence after the workings extended up to the foreshore. Here, the land above the old workings is beginning to flood.

3-7. A new lease in 1888 allowed the mine to extend out under the sea and, following an influx at high tide in 1898, it was quickly realised that a new sea defence would be needed. This was started in 1900, completed in 1905, and enclosed 170 acres (69 ha) of new land with rich deposits of ore under a shelf of limestone.

3-7 The Outer Barrier. September 1967

The new barrier was designed to be flexible, unlike the inner barrier, so that if subsidence should occur below the barrier it would sink in to fill any cavity formed. The superstructure could then be repaired to fill any deficit and protect the mine. The barrier was also to be of great weight so that it would compact the sand underneath and prevent water percolating below it. The barrier consists of a clay bank between two banks of rubble limestone all protected by blocks of limestone and concrete.

3-38. Steam powered Cornish beam engines were used to pump water from the mines. They were well-suited to the conditions, being able to remove sand and small pebbles as well as water. No. 8 pit (New Annie Lowther) was started in July 1897 and completed in November 1900. A 70 inch (1.78 m) pump, from Harvey and Company of Cornwall, was installed.

3-38 Annie Lowther, 8 & 10 Beam Houses. July 1967

No. 8 pit had levels at 40, 50, 60 and 70 fathoms and gave access to the area between the barriers. The pit was used mainly for raising ore.

3-45. The sinking of No. 10 pit began in June 1909 and was completed in 1910 to a depth of 70 fathoms (128 m). It acted as a replacement pumping shaft to Annie-Lowther pit. The boiler's chimney is on the left.

3-45 Hodbarrow No.10 Beam Engine + Lighthouse. Note headstock demolished. June 1968

3-47 (overleaf). This beam engine, made by Williams, Perran Foundry Co., Cornwall in 1878, operated until 1962. It had a 10 ft (3 m) stroke and was of 147.5 hp (1100 kW).

3-47 Hodbarrow No.10 Beam Engine assembly. October 1968

3-67 Moorbank Shaft Headstock, Hodbarrow. June 1968

3-67. A new reserve of haematite was discovered in the Moorbank area, inside the outer barrier, in 1925. The ore was in vein deposits at a depth of 90 fathoms (165 m). The deposit was too far from the existing shafts and so a new shaft No.11, or Moorbank, was sunk close to the western end of the outer barrier. Sinking started in the summer of 1928. Problems were encountered with water feeders and the shaft was not completed to its full depth of 586 ft (178 m) until 1931. It eventually became a separate mine, its connections back to the original mine being blocked, and pumping operations put in place. This was the last regularly worked part of the mine and a familiar sight to walkers and beach visitors at the Haverigg end of the Hodbarrow complex.

3-74. Moorbank shaft was electrically powered from the beginning; earlier shafts used steam powered winders. Electricity came from a 500 kW steam-turbine generator on the mine.

When Mike Davies-Shiel took his pictures of Hodbarrow Mines in 1967 and 1968, he captured the end of an era, as mining for iron ore was ending after more than a century, and demolition was underway on almost all of its industrial buildings. He seized an opportunity to go underground at Moorbank on February 19th 1968, a month before mining ceased with the loss of 103 jobs.

3-74 Winding engine house. (The operator is thought to be Jim Fawcett.) January 1968

The following pictures **3-75**, **3-77**, **3-81**, **3-82**, **3-84**, **3-91**, **3-94**, **3-95** illustrate how the mine operated in its final days. Note the red staining of all the equipment and people in the photographs, due to the haematite ore.

3-82 Hodbarrow Iron Mine. Empty ore bogies in the pit cage. 1968.

3-77 The mine manager, R B Davies, Moorbank Pit Head. February 19th 1968

3-75 Shaft signals. January 1968

3-81 Getting down ? feet. Mr R B Davies, Underground Manager. 19 February 1968

3-84. Underground haulage was by a continuous rope system. Because of the constant threat of flooding, all the engines were kept on the surface and the ropes descended the shafts and passed around a large pulley at the end of the drive as shown here.

3-84 Haulage Jack to 90 fathoms from the 85 fathom level. February 1968

3-91. Drilling holes in the ore face ready for blasting at Moorbank South. The miner is thought to be George Clampitt. He is using a drill powered by compressed air, but in the 19th century, the holes would have been made with a jumper and hammer.

3-91 Drilling for blasting. Moorbank South. February 19th 1968

3-94. A small loader mounted on rails, and powered by compressed air, could pick up ore in front of it and pass it over its own body into a tub behind.

3-94 Automatic ore loader (operated by Jimmy O'Brien). February 1968

3-95. Empty tubs were manually pushed from the end of the haulage system to the working face and full tubs returned again by hand.

3-95 A bogie man! February 19th 1968 (Les Nelson)

3-62 Snipey - with crane. July 1967

3-62. This Neilson's of Glasgow 0-4-0 crane locomotive, works number 4004, was nicknamed Snipey. It was delivered in 1890 and the driver's cab was originally open to the elements. It was used mainly for moving rails and timbers around the site. The locomotive went into preservation after the closure of Hodbarrow.

3-36 Surface mine tipper trucks near Arnold and Annie Lowther Pit-heads. October 1968

3-36. In the earlier days of the mines, much of the output left the site by sea from Borwick Rails harbour, in small coastal vessels, and these side-tipping pier wagons could load the boats. The containers were originally made of wood.

3-68 Loading the rail wagons. The lad loading road lorries. January 1968

3-26 Flooding of Hodbarrow. September 1969

3-26. Since the mines closed and pumping stopped, the area inside the outer barrier has been allowed to flood. The resulting 'coastal lagoon', still protected from the sea by the 1905 outer barrier, is an RSPB reserve and Site of Special Scientific Interest.

Backbarrow Iron Works

Backbarrow was the first of the newly designed blast furnaces to be built in the south of the county. Prior to this, iron ore had been processed into iron using various types of bloomery to produce a bloom of wrought iron.

It was built in 1711 by the Backbarrow Iron Company (William Rawlinson, John Machell and Stephen Crossfield were the principal partners). The blast furnace was a substantial stack of local stone close to a steep bank on which storehouses for iron ore and fuel were built, only a few steps lower than the bridge loft to the top of the furnace. This first furnace hearth was only 2 ft (0.6 m) square and 2 ft deep and produced 14.5 tons of iron per week. New hearths of increased size were built in 1770, 1888, 1911, 1927 and 1963, this last capable of producing 2,240 tons of cast iron per week.

A severe shortage of charcoal from the beginning of WW1 meant that Backbarrow could not produce the iron that would have been so valuable for armaments, and the furnace lay idle. The site was sold in 1917 to Augustus While and his brother, sons of J.M. While, a Darlington ironmaster who had been appointed General Manager of Barrow Haematite Iron & Steel Co. in 1891. By June 1919, the furnace had been re-lined, ore and charcoal stocks replenished, and the furnace went into blast. It continued as a profitable business, later managed by Dennis While, until 1966.

125-38 Backbarrow Iron Works built 1711. Oldest in country that is still in operation. Concrete posts + blocks for sale. Summer 1959

125-38. The tall, narrow chimneys mark the position of cupolas – tubular, vertical hearths, firebrick lined, which were used to produce cold-blast iron when the main furnace converted to hot-blast. Concrete, made from the accumulated slag mixed with Portland cement, was initially used on the site, and nearby, in the 1950s. Later, it was made for sale in the form of blocks.

125-19 Backbarrow. December 1966. Last at work on 23 February 1966.

125-19. The brick furnace stack is just to the left of centre of this photo, with the bridge crossing the road to the water-lift tower and the ore storage sheds to the right. The Lakeside and Haverthwaite railway runs above and behind the sheds, and trains delivered ore, coke and limestone from a purpose-built siding. The nearest buildings in the photo, called the pug mill, housed the turbines, a joinery workshop and the preparation area for the clay plugs used to block the flow of iron.

The blast furnace process at Backbarrow

The furnace would be operated continuously for 30 to 50 weeks, the period being termed a 'campaign'. The ore was mixed with limestone and, in the early days, cinders (bloomery slag, which could contain as much as 60% iron, and which also acted as a flux), and tipped into the top of the furnace with the fuel. Carbon, silica, sulphur, phosphorus or manganese might be added according to customer requirements. Air was blown into the hearth by paired bellows through apertures called tuyeres. The bellows were originally made from 15 -18 bulls' hides, and powered by a waterwheel, which was replaced in 1888 by water turbines backed up by a horizontal steam engine. Latterly, an electric compressor was used to provide the blast. After about 12 hrs the waste (slag) was tapped off and the liquid iron run into sand moulds (pigs), thus producing cast or 'pig' iron. Judging the right time to tap the furnace was the most skilled job.

125-128. Fuel (originally charcoal, but coke from 1927), iron ore and limestone (flux) needed to be added at the top of the furnace at frequent intervals. Initially it was carried to the top of the furnace in swill baskets, but the introduction of water-powered lifts in 1856 made it possible to use hand-carts holding four hundredweight (203 kg) of ore and fuel, as seen here.

125-128 Fred Booth recharging the furnace. December 1962

125-40 Backbarrow. Tapping the slag. December 1962

125-40. Slag is formed when the impurities contained in the iron ore combine with the limestone. It is less dense than the molten iron and floats on the top and so needed to be removed first.

87-95 Backbarrow. The ladle is nearly full. Mr E Baines (foreman) Tommy Baines, Fred Booth, Len Rogerson. December 1962

87-95. Note the apparent absence of protective gloves or headgear, apart from flat caps. Mike commented that they did not even have strong steel toe cap boots, although one of the commoner causes of injury was from dropping hot pigs of iron on their feet.

125-131 Backbarrow. Removing the slag before pouring. Tommy Baines. December 1962

125-131. The iron was originally tapped straight into the pig beds, but later it was tapped into a ladle to allow it to be poured either directly into moulds, or into the pig beds. Despite tapping the slag first, some still came out with the iron; this floated on the top of the ladle and could be raked off before pouring.

125-3 Backbarrow Crane Operator at work. 17 ton. Bob Dickinson [above] Tommy Baines [below]. December 1962

125-3. The first furnace was run by seven men – two founders, three fillers and two bridge servers who filled the baskets with fuel and ore. By the 1960s the expanded workforce included a crane operator and an analyst who sampled the iron.

*125-63 Backbarrow. Filling the pig beds (made from moulding sand).
Len Rogerson, Fred Booth. December 1962*

125-125 Backbarrow. Sand thrown onto pigs to cool, before breaking. December 1962

87-196 Backbarrow. The tap-hole stopper, Mr Len Rogerson. December 1962

125-64 Backbarrow. Blocking the flow of iron. Len Rogerson. December 1962

87-196 and **125-64**. Once the molten iron had been drawn off the furnace, the tap hole needed blocking to stop further iron escaping. This was done by forcing clay into the tap hole.

Note the furnace lintel recording the initials of the original owners (partly out of shot to the left) and Harrison Ainslie and Co., owners of Newland Furnace (near Ulverston) who had bought Backbarrow in 1818, to work in tandem with Newland. When one furnace was out of blast for relining with new firebricks, the other could be operating to supply their customers. Newland furnace ceased work in 1890.

125-69 (overleaf). The stockyard could hold 5,000 tons of pigs waiting to be dispatched to purchasers. Some continued to order the traditional pigs with stamped names such as Valley, Grazebrook, (**125-78**) but others specified a formula. It was not easy to control the composition of the furnace output to the exacting requirements of modern steelmakers and iron founders, so each batch was accompanied by a cast number burnt into a strip of wood which tallied with the formula in the analyst's records. Each stack of pigs would have a very slightly different chemical composition and they were selected to meet the purchaser's requirements, depending on the intended use of the iron. Customers included industrial giants such as Chrysler, Daimler, Austin, Singer Sewing Machines, Armstrong Whitworth, Vickers & Maxim and Woolwich Arsenal.

125-78 Backbarrow Pig stamps. September 1999

125-69 Backbarrow. Pig iron stockyard down to footbridge over the river. December 1962

Iron and Steel making at Moss Bay, Workington

Moss Bay has a long history of iron and steel making, and of the manufacture of rails. Barepot Ironworks opened in 1763. There followed a long and convoluted story of the various iron works opening, closing or being taken over; some disappeared entirely from the industrial scene, amalgamations saved others, but today there are none! The only exception is Tata Steel's engineering works (Distington Engineering). Wrought iron rails were made in the area from the earliest days and were superseded by steel rails, the first being rolled in 1877. They played a major role in the development of many of the world's railways, the name of Workington being synonymous with permanent way products and railway engineers. Improvements were continually made in rail quality and specifications to meet the ever more demanding and stringent conditions of international railways and high speed trains.

Steel was made using Bessemer converters and more recently electric arc furnaces. Rails were rolled using ingots from the Bessemer plant. These hot ingots could still be molten inside so had to be put in the soaking pit for 24 hours to ensure that they were at the correct and even temperature throughout before rolling. After the Bessemer plant closed in 1974, steel blooms were brought over from Teesside. Rolling was a multistage process, starting with the cogging mill, which reduced the cross section of the bloom and thereby lengthened it. It was then passed to the roughing mill and finally the finishing mill, making several passes through each. The last rail was rolled on 25th August 2006, after which rail rolling was moved to Scunthorpe.

Mike Davies-Shiel visited and recorded this area on a number of occasions, most recently in 2006 just prior to the closure

39-68 Workington. Teeming (pouring) the electric arc steel. February 1965

of the rail making works. What follows is a small selection of his photographs showing some of the processes.

Derwent Iron Works, Workington

The Derwent Works was on the original site of a blast furnace which was built in 1874 and was known as The Derwent Hematite Iron Co. By 1883 there were three furnaces in operation and the company was taken over by Charles Cammell & Co., who moved their subsidiary, Wilson, Cammell & Co., from Dronfield to Workington, including all the workforce and many of the townspeople as well. This brought the works close to a prime source of haematite and it was this company that erected the steelworks. Derwent Works closed on 23rd May 1981.

39-16 (overleaf). General view of the Derwent blast furnaces from the north. Furnaces No. 2, 3 & 4 are in the background (there was no No.1) with Cowper hot air stoves in the centre ground. The girder structure across the centre is part of the gantry for the pig iron stockyard crane, and in the foreground is a rake of pig iron wagons. The pig iron conveyor belt is the tall structure on the extreme right of the photograph. Blast furnaces produce iron from iron ore in a continuous process. The iron ore, coke (fuel) and limestone (flux) is fed into the top of the furnaces while a hot air blast that has been heated by exhaust gases from the furnaces is supplied into the bottom of the furnace through a series of pipes called tuyeres. This produces carbon monoxide, which reduces the iron ore to molten iron, which collected in the base of the furnace called the bosh with liquid slag on top. The molten iron was cast into iron products, e.g. pigs, and sold on to other manufacturers. At Workington the remainder would have been sent to the mixer at the steel making plant to be converted into steel in the Bessemer converter.

39-16 Blast furnaces, Workington. March 1963

39-14. No. 2 Furnace tapping slag. The impurities (slag) are run off first from the top of the iron through the slag-notch, which is the highest tapping point in the bosh. Once the slag has been removed that tapping point is sealed and the molten iron is tapped off from a lower point.

39-52. Tapping slag into a ladle at No. 2 Furnace. The ladle is then transported by rail to the slag bank.

39-70. These are empty iron ladles, used for transporting the molten iron to the mixer at the Bessemer steel making plant and also to the pig caster.

39-59. Molten iron being poured from an iron ladle into sand channels. It is then channelled into the pig caster conveyer.

39-11. View of furnaces and Cowper hot air stoves. The Cowper hot stoves are regenerating heat exchangers which use the hot flue gases from the furnace to heat up the blast air before it goes into the furnace. They contain refractory bricks stacked in an open chequer fashion. The hot gases from the furnace pass between the bricks and heat them up. Then cold air is passed through and is heated by the bricks before entering the furnace. Once the temperature of the bricks has fallen, the air is

39-14 Tapping the slag, Workington. November 1963.

43

39-52 Pouring slag, No. 2 furnace.
November 1963

39-70 Workington. January 1967.

39-59 Making cast iron pigs, Workington.
September 1962

39-11 Blast furnaces, Workington. 1964

shut off and the hot gases admitted and the whole process is repeated. The stoves work in pairs, so that one is heating up whilst the other is heating the air for the blast, ensuring a continuous supply of heated air.

39-10 Gas scrubbing plant. March 1967

39-10. The hot gases that are produced in the furnaces pass through this gas scrubbing plant, where impurities such as ammonia and tar are removed by 'washing' in water.

39-48. Coke is needed for smelting iron in the blast furnace and is made from coal by heating it in ovens in the absence of air. Coal gas, tar and ammonia are driven off and coke is left. Here coke is being pushed from the ovens into steel coke wagons before being quenched. A new battery of 53 Becker regenerative coke ovens was built in 1936 to replace those at Lowca, which was six miles away. This made the gas from the new ovens available for use in the steelworks and went some way to reducing the amount of coal used.

39-48 Workington. 60 tons red hot coke, being ejected into steel wagon. February 1965.

Steel Making, Workington

The Bessemer process was the first inexpensive industrial process for mass-production of steel from molten pig iron. Previously steel had been a specialist and costly metal used only for cutlery, springs, tools etc.

The principle involved is that of blowing air through molten iron to oxidise the impurities in the iron. The heat of the oxidation raises the temperature of the mass and keeps it molten during the operation. The converters are in two parts, an upper and a lower. Air is blown into the bottom of the vessel through tuyeres which are nozzles made of refractory material. They are housed in the 'plug' a component which wears very quickly and needs replacing after about 20 blows. To facilitate this it is held to the rest of the vessel with cotters.

39-20. The process was carried out at Workington in two 25 ton acid Bessemer converters. The converters have a steel shell which is lined with silica bricks and is called

39-20 Close-up of a Bessemer. New plant here in 1934. November 1963

39-21 The Bessemers. November 1963

39-26 Bessemer. Increasing the blast. February 1963

the vessel. It has a narrow upper end with an opening for charging with molten iron and for the finished product (steel) to be poured out. The bottom of the vessel is wider than the top and this is where the air is introduced through tuyeres and forced upwards and through the molten iron during the operation. The converter in action here is at the start of the blow, as seen by the short flame of a dull red colour.

39-21 (previous page). The blow is continuing, as can be seen by the change in the colour, but the flame is still only short. At the lower left of the picture the other vessel has been turned down for maintenance.

39-26. As the carbon in the molten iron begins to oxidise, it produces carbon monoxide, which burns to carbon dioxide as it comes into contact with atmospheric oxygen at the nose of the converter, causing the flame to lengthen and brighten until it is some 25 feet long and of intense brilliance.

39-25. The Bessemer vessel in motion. The casting crane with its hoisting beam and hooks can be seen silhouetted in the foreground. Just below and behind the hooks the teeming ladle is visible.

39-32 (overleaf). This shows the end of the blow and the vessel turning down to the horizontal. At the end of the blast, the clearing of the carbon is marked by the shortening of the flame, accompanied by an increase in the fume due to the oxidation of iron, which proceeds rapidly when the carbon has gone. This is the signal to turn the converter down to the horizontal position. The blast is left on during this movement until the molten steel is clear of the tuyeres, allowing the blast to clear the holes in the tuyeres of any molten metal. The blast is then shut off.

39-34 (overleaf). The molten steel is being poured into moulds. When cooled, the ingot will be removed from the mould and transported to the soaking pits before being rolled.

39-25 Workington. Bessemer. Rocking the mixture. February 1963.

39-32 The end of the blast. February 1963

39-34 Teeming the ingots. November 1963.

Rolling mill & rail finishing department, Workington

The first rails were rolled on this site in 1877 and over the years many modifications were made. One major event was the replacement of all the main drive steam engines with electric motors in 1956. The steel ingots came from the Bessemer plant and could still be molten inside when they arrived at the mill, so had to be placed in 'soaking pits'. Their purpose was to heat soak the ingots to ensure they were an even temperature throughout before they were transferred to the cogging mill for the first stage of rolling.

After the Bessemer steel plant closed in 1974 and the electric arc furnace in 1975, the soaking pits became redundant and were demolished. Instead, in 1973, a walking beam bloom reheating furnace was installed to re-heat blooms brought over from Teesside, from ambient temperature to approximately 1250°C. This took between two and two and a half hours. The furnace held 67 blooms and was fired by natural gas, but oil firing could be used if necessary.

39-37 Workington. Ingot lifted from Soaking Pit after 24 hours. February 1967.

39-37. This shows an ingot being lifted out of the soaking pits with the tongs crane and being transported to the cogging mill. The soaking pits were built in 1935, when the 25 ton Bessemer converters were installed, and were refractory lined and heated with coke oven gas.

39-91 Hot bloom approaching cogging mill on in-going table. February 2006.

39-91. Here a heated bloom from the walking beam furnace approaches the cogging mill for the first stage in the rolling process. The bloom is on the in-going main table and in between the manipulators that were used to move the bloom across the main table for each pass through the rolls. The kicker legs can be seen which were used to turn the bloom through 90° as required during the rolling process. Depending on the order, there would be five or seven passes through the rolls. The bloom was by now much longer and thinner, but in the process the ends would often have become deformed or damaged and were cut off in the shears. The still hot steel was then moved to the roughing mill to start the process of forming the desired rail profile. The movement of the bloom through the rolls was controlled from a cabin on a gantry (**39-93** overleaf).

39-93 The cogging driver, Alan White, in his cabin behind a double thickness of armoured glass. February 2006

39-95. Roughing rolls are on the right, with a part-formed rail going into the rolls for the second pass. It required five passes through the roughing rolls before the part-formed rail would be pushed over to the finishing rolls by wire rope-operated skids. To complete the finished rail required four more passes through the finishing rolls. The rail exiting the finishing rolls is on the last pass and will be branded on the underside of the rail. Branding includes rail mill, section, grade and year rolled. At this point the rail is still at about 1000 - 1100°C.

39-105. The rails were cut to the required length and then transferred to the cooling banks, using skids and a roller table. Here the rails cooled from about 900°C to ambient temperature in about 4 hours. Due to the section of the finished rail, with more material in the head than in the flange, cooling took place at different speeds and caused the rail to curve one way and then the other. To assist in keeping the rail straight, the pushers on the cooling banks would be set at different cambers. The cooling banks were over 70 metres long.

39-95 Workington. Rolling mills in action. March 1967.

39-105 Workington. Rails cooling. November 1963.

39-107. Finally, rails still needed to be accurately straightened by passing through in-line dual plane (vertical and horizontal) straightening rolls. There was a large demand for high quality rails from all over the world, requiring great precision in this operation.

39-107 Vertical straightener on cold rail. February 2006.

39-108 Finished products. All sizes of rail. February 1963.

39-111 shows a small selection of the products rolled in the mill's later years. At the top are five rows of shaft guide rails for the National Coal Board. These needed to be ultra-straight and, as they were not in great demand, were not a very profitable line. The rest of the stock is railway track of varying profiles. The middle row of bull-head rail was probably for London Underground, at that time the main UK users of this rail. The remainder of the rail is the flat-bottomed type, in general use, but rolled in a variety of weights and profiles. The squat rails at the centre of the bottom row could have been conductor rails for third rail electric lines such as those south of London. The heavier profile rails at the bottom right have wider bases and were probably for use as runners for overhead cranes.

39-111 Bull head + other rails. February 2006

Foundries

The early foundries were closely associated with the small blast furnaces in the Furness area, but as iron production increased rapidly due to the larger coke-fired furnaces, many small independent foundries were established in the towns. Their cast iron (and, later, steel) products were widely used in the home, in agriculture, on the railways, and in local industry where cast iron was replacing wood in mill wheels and machinery. The products ranged from the purely functional (**114-145**, **303-20**) to the decorative and fanciful (**124-25** - Page 56).

303-20 Gilkes, Kendal. 2007

303-20. Gilkes' foundry was principally part of their turbine manufacturing business, but the firm was also one of several Kendal foundries that made gulley grates and drain covers, and was the last Kendal firm to do so, not closing their foundry until 1960.

125-194. This Penrith foundry remained in the Stalker family for nearly 120 years from 1851, specialising in agricultural engineering, threshing machines etc, until it was sold to a Kirkby Thore haulier who, in 1974, turned the Castlegate premises into a working steam museum. In 1994 the valuable steam traction engines and other exhibits were sold at a public auction.

114-145 Cottage fireplace at High Hall Garth, Little Langdale.

114-145. Note the 'fire crane', a pivoting bar from which the 'ratten crooks' of different lengths were suspended to hold the pans over the fire. Hot water could be drawn from the tap at the bottom left.

125-194 Agricultural machinery by Stalker Bros. of Penrith at Loweswater. September 1993

8-148 Cast iron building on Branthwaite Brow, Kendal, b. 1853. April 1990

8-148. Joseph Winder of Kendal's Lound Foundry made the decorated cast iron plates which are suspended on the timber frame of this frontage, supposedly to minimise the projection of the building into the narrow street.

302-36. Built as a foundry in the late 18th or early 19th century, this listed building has the arched 'Gothic' windows which Mike identified as being typical of foundries, especially in West Cumbria, leading the uninitiated to suppose they had been built as chapels. By the time of the first Ordnance Survey maps, it had become a steam sawmill, but later reverted to metal-working when the engineering firm of Joseph Pirt took over the building in 1913. They undertook several important Admiralty contracts during both World Wars. In the 1960s Joseph Pirt & Co advertised themselves as Ship Repairers, Mechanical and Electrical Engineers, undertaking boiler work, copper pipe work, welding and forging.

206-9. To make a casting, the founder might use scrap metal as well as 'virgin' material such as cast iron pigs, and it would appear that this was the case here. Pratchitt's Foundry was established in 1859 on Long Island in Carlisle, and moved in 1863 to Denton Holme. Their speciality was making steam pumps and stationary steam engines. More recently, combining with the Manchester firm of L.A. Mitchell, they specialised in industrial dryers.

They were one of a number of foundry and engineering firms that were established in Carlisle in the early 19th century to provide a service to the local textile and railway industries. One of the most famous was Cowans Sheldon who started producing castings for railway engines and wagons, both men having been trained as apprentices in railway works in the north-east. However the firm quickly moved into crane production both stationary, and for railways.

302-36 Pirt's foundry, Church St., Workington. 2007

206-9 Pratchitt's Foundry, Carlisle. c. 1967

8-209 Iron Foundry gate post, Cartmel, by Middleton of Kendal, Ironmongers. November 1984

124-25 Cast iron work by Mr Pittard the younger, on pipe at Natland Foundry. October 1992

124-25. Natland Foundry was reputedly one of the first in Cumbria, being set up at the instigation of Isaac Wilkinson of Wilson House, Lindale, in the mid 18th century, to make his newly designed cast iron smoothing irons.

In an 1885 Kendal directory, William Middleton is recorded as an "Ironmonger and Iron and Fencing Manufacturer". The gatepost in **8-209** is at Cartmel, but others of the same design can be found elsewhere in South Lakeland with associated iron fencing. There is still a Middleton's ironmonger's shop in Kendal.

125-122. This decorative cast iron grille, which Mike said was the second best in Europe, has now been replaced by a modern wooden floor.

125-122 Cast iron at its best at St Mary's Church, Ambleside, Lonsdale F(oundry?). June 1965

WATER POWER

Water was the most important source of power in Cumbria from Roman times until the end of the 19th century. This power was harnessed via waterwheels which were used to provide power in a wide range of industries. Corn mills are the classic example, but they were also used in metal working, both mining and processing, and textiles. It was the availability of a suitable water supply that determined the siting of mills, which might change their function over the years from, for example, fulling mill to woollen mill, to paper or bobbin mill.

The size and type of waterwheel depended on the rate of flow that could be maintained, and the height of fall above the wheel. The simplest form of wheel had paddles on it and this type was simply suspended in a stream so that the flow turned the wheel (undershot wheel) (**22-127**). Undershot wheels are not particularly efficient but were widely used in lowland areas of Cumbria where it is difficult to get sufficient fall for other forms of wheel. Efficiency was increased by a closely fitting wheelpit and sometimes wheels had clearances of less than 1/4 inch (0.6 cm).

22-127 Undershot waterwheel, Low Goat Mill, Cockermouth. 1850s cast iron replacement into 1750s fabric. March 1972

The majority of waterwheels have a series of buckets around the rim which hold the water and it is the weight of water on the wheel that provides the power. Depending on the amount of fall available, the water usually falls onto the wheel at half the height of the wheel (mid breast wheel) or between there and the top of the wheel as at Hawkshead Hill (**1-127**). Earlier waterwheels were mainly made of wood, which was often later replaced with cast iron.

1-127 Hawkshead Hill Bobbin Mill, mid-high breast waterwheel. November 1967

1-127. Hawkshead Hill, also known as Thursgill Mill, had a 26 ft (7.9 m) diameter, 2.25 ft (0.69 m) wide waterwheel. Waterwheels varied greatly in diameter and width, the largest mostly constructed for pumping water from mines and to drive textile mill machinery. Corn mill waterwheels were generally somewhat smaller.

14-117 Kirkoswald Corn Mill. September 1979

12-29. Witherslack Corn Mill. Pitchback 22 x 2.5 ft. Note cast iron starter box. 1964.

The water can either go across the top of the wheel and the wheel rotates in the direction of the water flow (overshot) (**14-117**), or can go onto the wheel just before top and the wheel rotates against the direction of flow of the water (pitchback) (**12-29**). Overshot wheels were less suitable where the water flow was variable and prone to flooding because the bottom of the wheel was rotating against the flow of water in the watercourse.

In the middle of the 19th century there were improvements in the use of water power with the development of Pelton wheels and turbines. Both of these use the force of water hitting a rotor rather than the weight of water actually on the wheel.

55-27 Francis turbine at Stocks Bobbin Mill, Skelsmergh. August 1964

The development of turbines coincided with the development of electricity as a power supply. So not only were they used to drive machinery directly (**55-27**), they were also connected to dynamos to produce

29-96 Hydro-electric power at Haverthwaite. GG&G turbine no.5207. March 1965

Keswick, Coniston and Troutbeck Bridge. The creation of the National Grid and nationalisation reduced the number and variety of generating plants, but recent government renewable energy incentives have encouraged the installation of turbines for small scale hydro-electricity generation, with surplus electricity sold to the power supply companies.

29-96. In 1952, two Gilkes turbines were installed at the former Lowwood Gunpowder works, Haverthwaite, to generate electricity for the National Grid, taking advantage of the existing weir and mill race previously used in gunpowder manufacture. These have recently been replaced with two Archimedean screw turbines.

electricity (**29-96**). Small independent units provided electricity for individual country houses while larger installations generated power for communities, for example, at

83-75 Main turbine construction shed at Gilkes Canal Head works, Kendal. 1964

83-75. Turbine manufacture at Canal Head, Kendal started with the Williamson brothers, agricultural engineers, in 1856. By the time the company was bought by Gilbert Gilkes in 1881, they had built 439 turbines. Gilkes, later Gilbert Gilkes & Gordon, continued to specialise in custom made turbine installations for very many of the local industries, country houses including Balmoral Castle and Sir Thomas Armstrong's Cragside, and for export, and now claims to be the largest manufacturer in the UK of turbines up to 20 MW.

CORN MILLING & BREWING

Most grains need to be processed after harvesting before they can be consumed by humans or most farm animals. Grains are covered by a protective hull which has to be either broken or removed completely to allow access to the nutritious starches and proteins inside. This was originally done by hand, first using rubbing stones and later using hand powered querns (**12-5**). The problem with hand milling was that it was slow and only small quantities of grain could be processed.

The grain most commonly grown in Cumbria was oats, and the ground oatmeal was mixed with water to make porridge or oatcakes.

12-5 Hand quern stone found near Whitebeck Mill, Burton. October 1980

Milling

As the milling process became mechanised, milling was transferred from the home to a specific building - the corn mill, powered either by wind or water. Because processed grain was a staple of most people's diets, and was also important for animal feeds, most parishes had at least one corn mill; Cumbrian topography and climate meant that the majority were watermills, but there were at least 30 windmill sites in Cumbria (**300-233**).

Once a suitable site had been found for a watermill, with a sufficient head of water to drive a waterwheel, and suitable access to allow grain to be delivered to the mill, it was used for centuries. Many mills were rebuilt on the site several times as a result of being destroyed by fire, flooding, or to increase the size of the mill, or to introduce new machinery. What the power of the water was used for changed at some sites depending on wider economics and local demand for different products, as technologies and industries changed. Fulling, bobbin making, flax processing, paper making and other industries have all been carried out on former corn milling sites.

300-233 Wigton windmill and kiln shed or drying house. September 1971

225-1 Goat mill, Cockermouth.

225-1. Low Gote Mills. (The area on the north bank of the Derwent to the west of Cockermouth has been known at various times as Goat or Gote and the name appears interchangeable over time.)

A corn mill was built on the site in 1609, although there is documentary evidence for milling before that. According to a map of 1727, there were three mills on the site, labelled Logwood Mill, Wheat Mill and Corn Mill. The mills were rebuilt in 1779 as textile mills and it is probably at this period that the site was reduced to two mills: the upper mill, pictured here, and the lower mill, which has been demolished. A map of 1832 labels both as flax mills, with the upper mill owned by Thomas Mawson and lower by Jonathan Harris.

By the time of the 1st edition Ordnance Survey map, 1863, both mills had been converted back to corn mills.

The upper mill was converted to a private house in 1978.

Grain needs to be dry (below 14% moisture) before it can be milled successfully into a flour. In Cumbria, due to the weather, it is usually not possible to harvest grain with a low enough moisture content to allow it to be milled directly. Therefore most corn mills in Cumbria had an associated corn drying kiln. These were either stand-alone buildings, or were attached to the mill. They usually consisted of an inverted cone within the building, with a small hearth at the bottom. The top of the cone would be

19-86 Thwaites Mill, near Millom. Barley kiln tiles. February 1966

covered with a mesh supported on either a wooden or metal frame. The grain was spread on the mesh and a small fire was lit in the hearth at the bottom. The hot air was drawn up through the grain and there was some form of cowl on the roof to cause a draw and remove the smoke from the kiln.

Originally the mesh was a coarse blanket, but with improvements in transport, perforated clay tiles (as shown in **19-86**), laid on iron bars became available and were of a lower fire risk. The grain would require regular turning to allow even drying and long handled wooden shovels were used (**121-279**).

121-279 Kirksanton corn mill. Kiln shovel and barrel. February 1986

Corn mills work by grinding the grain between two millstones. The lower stone (bedstone) is fixed and the upper stone (runner) rotates above it. Both stones are slightly curved, the bedstone being convex and the runner concave. The gap between them gets narrower towards the outside but the stones do not touch. Each stone has a series of furrows carved into it. The furrows that pass the full width of the stone are known as master furrows; the furrows branching off the master furrows are known as slave furrows. The areas of stone between the furrows are known as the land.

Grain falls between the two stones in the centre, is caught in the master furrows and is dragged towards the outside of the stone. As the gap between the stones gets narrower the grain is slowly broken and is then forced along the slave furrows before finally passing through the narrowest gap between the lands and being pushed out of the outside edge as flour.

43-14 Stone floor at Crosthwaite, Lyth. French Burr (on left). June 1966

43-14. This picture shows the 3 bedstones at Crosthwaite Mill – 2 grit and 1 French burr, fastened to the floor. The drive shaft passed up through the bedstones and the runner was suspended from it. The whole was encased in a wooden case, the tun.

Gritstone from the Pennines was most commonly used for millstones in the early mills, being best suited for oats and barley. From the mid-18th century French burrs were imported, made from quartz from the Marne valley in northern France. They were made up of small pieces held together by an iron band and backed with plaster-of-Paris. These very hard (and expensive) stones were used for milling wheat.

In the Lake District local stone was also used, including Eskdale, Shap and Ennerdale granites, and Lazonby sandstones.

83-25 Cracking a French burr at Muncaster Mill, Ravenglass. John Fairbanks. May 1977

300-414 Gears at Little Salkeld corn mill. June 1989

After milling about 100 tons of grain, the stones would need dressing. This involved roughening the surfaces and 'cracking' the furrows. It might be done by an expert millwright such as John Fairbanks (**83-25**), or by a team of skilled 'cadgers' who travelled around the mills, or by the miller himself, although it was difficult for one man to lift and work on the stones safely.

300-414. The majority of the machinery in corn mills was made from locally grown timber. Wood had the advantage that there was no chance of sparks (as could occur with iron machinery), which could cause an explosion due to all the flour dust in the mill. Also, if the machinery became jammed, wooden cogs would break without causing irreparable damage.

*19-40 Muncaster Mill.
Derby grit re-cracked. May 1977*

The picture shows the great spur wheel (large wheel at top). This engages with the stone nuts (small wheels next to it) to transfer the drive to the runner stone. The drive from the waterwheel is transferred to the great spur wheel via the pitwheel and the wallower (**50-31**). In this example it is a lantern wheel instead of the more common cog wheel seen in **300-414**.

The pitwheel turned at the same speed as the waterwheel, between 2.5 and 10 rpm, typically 7 rpm. The wallower (due to its smaller number of cogs) and the great spurwheel then turned approximately three times as fast, and further gearing drove the stones 5.5 times as fast again, giving the average runner stone a speed in the region of 115 rpm.

300-291 Crosthwaite corn mill. Details of worm gear on stone crane. July 1991

300-291. Fine workmanship in wood. The stone crane was used to raise the runner stone to allow it to be dressed.

50-31 Newby Bridge Corn Mill. Pitwheel & lantern wallower. September 1992

Local watermills stayed in use until steam power was developed and there was a change from milling with stones to the use of rollers. The use of local wheat to produce flour for bread came to an end with the introduction of cheaper and better quality wheat from overseas. This wheat arrived at the ports, where large steam powered mills were built, for example Silloth (**7-199**) and Barrow. The local mill in some cases continued to process other grains for animal feed, but this was eventually centralised in large factories.

215-37. Jonathan Dodgson Carr, a Quaker from Kendal, set up a bakery and flour mill in Carlisle in 1831. His business rapidly expanded and he built this factory to mass produce biscuits using machinery modelled on printing press designs. At this stage, biscuits were made simply from flour and water, hence 'Carr's Water Biscuits', for which he received a Royal Warrant, but he went on to develop many varieties of 'fancy' biscuits such as custard creams, bourbons, jam rings etc. These were sold as assortments packed in tins made by the nearby Carlisle firm of Hudson Scott & Sons (the Metal Box Co. from 1921). Many of the same biscuit varieties are still made by the million in this factory under the McVities label in spite of severe flooding in 2005 and 2015.

7-199. Built as a steam-powered roller flour mill in 1887 by Jonathan Dodgson Carr, a computerised animal feed compound plant was added in 1963. Grain from Canada and elsewhere could be vacuum-pumped directly from dockside ships into the mill. From its installation in 1905 until 1973, a magnificent Belgian, coal-powered, Carel steam engine drove the various plant processes and generated electricity via its giant flywheel and belts. Although it was retired in favour of oil-fired generators and pneumatic plant, it is still preserved and is occasionally demonstrated to the public.

215-37 Carr's Works, Caldewgate, Carlisle. Built 1837.

7-199 Silloth Dock Flour Mills. 1978

Brewing

Grain, mainly barley, is also used for brewing. Prior to the 19th century, most beer was brewed in the home, but with the Industrial Revolution medium-sized and, increasingly, large businesses moved into the local towns, brewed the beer and managed the pubs and bars. More recently, new small scale independent breweries have started up, encouraged by CAMRA, the Campaign for Real Ale.

201-3. The first stage in brewing is malting. The grain is soaked in water and then spread out on the malting floor for the seeds to start germinating, beginning the conversion of starch to sugar. After a few days the process is halted by heating in the kiln. The resulting 'malt' is milled and then mixed with hot water in the 'mash tun', allowing the enzymes in the malt to continue the process of turning starch into fermentable sugar. After boiling with hops, the 'wort' is cooled and yeast added to start the fermentation which produces the alcohol.

201-3 Malthouse, Grizebeck

The advent of the First World War saw the building of the munitions factory known as ROF (Royal Ordnance Factory) in the Gretna area, just over the Scottish border. It brought a large number of workers for its construction and 15,000 for employment in the factory, many of whom had to be housed in Carlisle and the surrounding area. These workers had a disposable income and Carlisle was the place where a lot of it was spent. This led to a significant increase in drunkenness, especially at weekends, and reduced productivity on Monday mornings. As a result the Central Control Board (Liquor Traffic) was formed in 1915. This nationalised brewing and retailing in

16-146 Carlisle's District State Managed Brewery, display of crates. May 1989

areas of important munitions production across the country. Under these controls, Carlisle's four breweries were nationalised, together with 400 public houses in Carlisle and Maryport districts. The New, Queen's and High Breweries were all closed down, and production was centralised at the Old Brewery (**16-146** and **226-2**). By 1918, nearly half of all Carlisle's licensed premises had been shut. In 1921, the Central Control Board was taken over by the State Management Scheme, which continued to manage brewing and public houses in Carlisle until abolished by Act of Parliament in 1971.

23-41. This former water-powered corn mill, said to date back to 1671, became a brewery about 1860, using locally grown barley, and hops from Pontefract. The square building in the centre with the vent on the roof top is the old malthouse. It had ceased production in World War I when the building was used instead for crushing and drying barytes from local mines. When this photo was taken in 1986 it was being converted into housing.

226-2 Malthouse and kiln, New Brewery, Carlisle. c. 1969

226-2. This site in Caldewgate, Carlisle was the New Brewery, which opened in 1778. It was closed when the state took over the Carlisle breweries in 1915, but continued as the maltings for the Old Brewery nearby. The site was cleared in 1974.

23-41 Caldbeck Brewery. April 1986

250-63. Founded in 1828 at the small village of Lorton, near Cockermouth, the expanding brewery moved into the town in 1874, to a site near the confluence of the Rivers Derwent and Cocker. Jennings was bought out in 2005 by Marstons, who own 5 breweries around the country and have 1,700 bars and pubs, but Jennings continues to brew a range of ales using the same traditional methods and water from its own well.

250-63 Jennings Brewery, Cockermouth.

22-63 Jennings van, Cockermouth Brewery, at Caldbeck. May 1987

13-132 Highgate Brewery, Kendal. August 1959

13-132. Kendal's Highgate Brewery was built by Whitwell Mark & Co in 1853 in the garden of the Georgian town house they had been using for their wine business since 1757. Brewing soon became the main focus of their activity and they bought up a number of local inns, such as the Cock & Dolphin and the Duke of Cumberland, becoming one of Kendal's major employers.

In 1946 they were taken over by Vaux Breweries and in 1971 the offices were relocated to Sunderland. 120 Highgate became a Youth Hostel, and the industrial buildings were converted into the Brewery Arts Centre.

45-83. Brewing on this site close to Ulverston town centre dates from 1755, using water taken from a well in the brewery yard. During the 19th century it was developed as a traditional Victorian tower brewery, powered by steam. After a number of changes of ownership it was bought in 1896 by the brothers Robert and Peter Hartley of Burnley, and Hartley's Brewery as it was famously known continued in production until 1991, although bought out by Robinson's of Stockport in 1982. The tall boiler house chimney was demolished in 1994, but most of the other buildings survive although the owners have permission to clear and re-develop the site for retail use.

45-83 Hartley's Brewery, off Soapery Lane, Ulverston. March 1998

SNUFF

Kendal's long association with tobacco and snuff has been attributed to its position on the 18th century packhorse routes from Whitehaven and Maryport. Snuff-taking has been considered less hazardous to health than smoking tobacco products, and it was widely used in dusty factories and mines, where smoking was banned for safety reasons. By the time these photos were taken, the snuff industry was in decline, although three of the remaining six snuff companies in the country were in Kendal and two of them, confusingly, carried the name of Gawith.

Samuel Gawith & Co were operating at The Brown House, Canal Head North, having given up their water-powered mills at Meal Bank, near Kendal and Eamont Bridge, near Penrith.

Illingworth's, which had been a large cigarette producer as well as making snuff, was also on Canal Head North, at Aynam Mills, until February 1983, when a major fire destroyed the property and machinery. Although snuff-making was soon re-started at Beezon Road, they closed in 1986.

Gawith, Hoggarth & Co had the snuff mill at Helsington Laithes, on the southern outskirts of Kendal, and the Gawith family premises at 27 Lowther St., with its distinctive "Turk" trade sign. (**43-75**)

43-75 Gawith Hoggarth's packing department, Lowther St, Kendal. October 1964

76-51 Helsington Laithes Snuff Mill, general view. October 1964

58-34 Helsington Laithes. One of four pestles. February 1991

From 1297, the River Kent had powered a corn mill at Helsington Laithes, on the southern boundary of Kendal. In 1800, two separate mills were built on the then ruinous site by Francis Webster, the architect, to saw and polish imported stone and local limestone, to make 'marble'.

In the 1880s Gawith, Hoggarth & Co took over the sawmill, with its undershot waterwheel, for the purpose of grinding and mixing snuff (**76-51**). By the time it closed in 1991, it was one of the last industrial sites in the country powered by a waterwheel.

The snuff-making process started with the careful selection and drying of tobacco leaf and stalks to suit the brand of snuff. To the right of centre in **76-51**, is a mechanised iron pestle and mortar which was used to grind the coarser, moist types of snuff. To the left of centre is a roller mill barrel where tennis-sized steel balls were rotated for the initial grinding of fine, dry snuffs, taking 10 hours to process 100 lb (45 kg) of tobacco. Further grinding used iron pestles in traditional oak mortars (**58-34** and **13-231**). (Illingworth's management were clearly more safety conscious.)

13-231 Snuff grinder set at Illingworth's. December 1964

The grinding processes were followed by sieving (**242-37**) to produce the base snuff or snuff 'flour', which was stored in barrels and left to mature. At 27 Lowther Street, various flavourings were added before packing in small tins (**58-48**).

Since the closure of Helsington Laithes mill, the firm of Gawith Hoggarth & Co no longer grinds snuff at Kendal, but uses imported base snuff powder to mix with a wide range of flavourings at their modern premises on the northern outskirts of town. Their website advertises 95 different varieties of snuff, as well as some pipe tobacco and also seven varieties of twist chewing tobacco.

58-76 Different sizes of sieve, February 1991

242-37 Sieve and jigger tray. Helsington Laithes.

58-48 Snuff tin samples at Helsington Laithes Mill. February 1991

58-46 Kendal Brown snuff, original label, Helsington Laithes. February 1991

WOODLAND AND ASSOCIATED INDUSTRIES

Use of timber for construction, firewood, and especially to make charcoal for bloomeries, led to the clearance of much of Cumbria's native woodland by medieval times, but gradually the need for a policy of forest conservation and management was recognised. New woodlands were planted, and existing supplies were safeguarded by coppicing. This was the practice of producing a sustainable crop of timber from broad-leaved woodland. A few trees, mostly oak, might be left to grow to full size as 'standards' for eventual use in construction as house or boat timbers.

Coppice wood was often sold as standing timber, by the acre, and a team of woodsmen were then contracted to do the coppicing.

Most Cumbrian woodland became very neglected in the 1970s and 80s, but recently there has been increased interest in managing woodlands to produce a crop, due to the expanding sales of wood-burning stoves, and to provide local charcoal for barbecues.

114-147. Coppice wood is produced by cutting trees almost to ground level. This encourages new growth of several stems from the stool (stump) ready for harvesting in 10 to 20 years' time. Coppicing tends to produce straight poles with little branching, with the advantage of having few knots, and being easy to handle and stack. The cut stools of most species produce up to twenty poles, but old lime tree stools may produce 100 or more (**250-64**).

114-147 Coppicing Swallowmire Wood, Cartmel Fell. February 1995

250-64 Lime coppice, Sayles, near Lowick Bridge. June 1989

Uses of coppice wood

Coppice wood had a wide variety of uses, some being sold with little further manufacturing, such as the twiggy growth of birch coppice, which was used to make hurdles for racecourses, fenders for ships (**62-26**) and besoms for domestic and industrial use (**9-65**). Thicker birch stems, along with other woods, were widely used in the local bobbin mills.

9-65 (overleaf). Besoms are generally thought of as a garden tool, good for sweeping leaves from the lawn, but bundles of birch twigs were used in large quantities by steel rolling mills to loosen and remove the iron oxide scale during the hot rolling process. Usually they were thrown on as the slab entered the roll bite but for long products a broom of twigs was held onto the

62-26 Richard Taylor - coppice cutter at Newby Bridge. Bundles of 25 into Ties of 4 for Liverpool Docks fenders. August 1960

9-65 J. Martindale, Besom maker for Carron Steel works, Scotland, at Dale Park, Rusland. 500 dozen per week. March 1971

9-104 Barrels. Old hazel hooped type at Grassguards, Dunnerdale. March 1974

bar and burnt away as the twigs removed the scale. High pressure water jets are now used for this purpose.

9-104. Coopering was a highly skilled craft which used coppice wood to make barrels for the local gunpowder industry (**30-86**), domestic and agricultural use and for breweries. Barrels to hold liquids were usually made with oak staves, which had to be carved very exactly to provide watertight joints.

30-86 Gunpowder keg, Threlkeld Quarry. May 2004

Basket-making

The traditional local basket, known as a swill, is still made today from coppiced oak and hazel. Hardwearing and long-lasting, swill baskets were used in local industries as well as on farms and in gardens.

62-75 Oak spelk/swillmaker, taws first, spells second! Mr Wilmot of Ulverston at Backbarrow. October 1963

62-75. The rim, or bool of the swill is made from hazel, steamed or boiled so that it can be bent to shape. The rest of the basket is made by weaving thin strips of oak split from coppice wood (**62-66**) and shaped as in **62-73**. The basket-maker sits astride the 'mare' or shaving bench and the spells or taws are held by a foot-operated clamp while they are being shaped.

62-66 Swill-making, Lowick Green. Use lat-axe, to rive into thinner pieces, c.1cm. June 1965

62-73. Swill-making, Lowick Green. Sit on mare to pare sides of spells or taws & shape ends. June 1965

62-54 William Hartley, Basket Maker, Eskdale. April 1970

62-54. This display of baskets for sale at Eskdale Green was a tourist attraction for a number of years, although it is uncertain to what extent the raw materials were locally produced by the time this picture was taken. The property, Moor Head, had been in the Hartley family at least since 1829, when Joseph Hartley was described as a "Joiner etc".

Clog-making

219-4 R. Brew's clog shop, Roper St, Whitehaven. March 1971

219-4. Clogs made from alder or sycamore soles, with leather uppers, were commonly worn by miners, factory workers, farmers and children. In the days before rubber boots, they kept feet dry in muddy conditions and were often stuffed with straw for added warmth.

Bobbin Mills and Wood turning

In the latter part of the 18th century, the earliest bobbin mills in the area started to produce bobbins for the local cotton carding mills. Barley Bridge (Staveley) for example, had its own bobbin mill in an adjacent building. However, as the Lancashire cotton industry flourished and the local cotton mills shut down, millions of bobbins were sent by train to the industrial towns, each cotton mill having its own particular requirements. By the second half of the 19th century there were 79 bobbin mills operating in Cumbria. After 1900, demand began to decline as the cotton mill owners got together to standardise bobbin sizes and knot-free Scandinavian timber lent itself to more automated production, so the orders went to larger steam-powered mills elsewhere. The local bobbin mills diversified, making various products with their wood-turning equipment and skills, until the last one closed in 1992.

55-19. Former bobbin mills can often be identified by their coppice wood drying sheds – open sided with the roof supported

55-19 Oakbank Mill, Skelsmergh coppice barn pillars pre 1851.

by stone pillars, cylindrical in the case of those built before about 1850 and square in section for the later ones.

1-241. Products of some of the South Lakeland mills showing reels (made from a single piece of wood), bobbins (constructed from more than one piece) and various other turned objects. Paxton's Mill at Staveley specialised in door knobs, Spark Bridge made parts for children's toys and had a brief boost to their profitability in 1935 when there was a craze for yo-yos. Stott Park

1-241 Bobbins, reels and other goods. November 1988

obtained a contract to provide toggles for duffel coats and rope ladder rungs for the Royal Navy. Other mills produced shafts for hammers, axes, spades etc.

43-84 Stott Park Bobbin Mill, Finsthwaite, built 1834. March 1967

43-84. In this photo, taken at the end of the winter, the yard is full of coppice wood ready to be stacked in the drying shed for seasoning. Silver birch, ash, sycamore, alder and rowan were all suitable for bobbin making, but not oak.

Most bobbin mills were converted from other water-powered mills, many on former fulling mill sites. Stott Park, however, was built on a new site and the substantial reservoirs at High Dam constructed to provide a reliable water supply for its waterwheel, soon replaced by a turbine made by Williamsons of Kendal. A series of dry summers in the 19th century led many mills to install a steam engine to run the mill when drought restricted the use of turbines. At Stott Park it could be used to drive one of the two turning sheds' shafts while the turbine drove the other. Electric power was installed in the 1940s.

Stott Park Bobbin Mill closed in 1971 and reopened in 1983 as a working museum, now run by English Heritage.

43-85. In all the local bobbin mills, power from a waterwheel, turbine or steam engine drove a central shaft with canvas belts

43-85 Stott Park. Typical line-shafting, main turning shed interior. March 1967

linking each machine to a drum on the shaft. Sometimes it was necessary, when a machine was not in use, to "knock off" the belt from the drum onto a light framework to prevent it from dropping onto the revolving shaft. Fitting the belt back onto the revolving drum was a difficult and hazardous process, but stopping the drive to the shaft would mean a financial loss for employees as well as employer since most were paid on a piecework basis.

1-99 Oakbank, Skelsmergh. Lengths for plugs. November 1964

55-89 Braithwaite borer, Finsthwaite. March 1967

1-99. Large timbers like this would be cut into slices called 'cakes' and a tubular 'blocking' saw (**51-74**) used to cut out as many pieces as possible. Waste wood and shavings were used to fire the boiler for the drying kiln.

55-89. Boring a central hole in the block was one of the early stages in the creation of a bobbin or reel. 'Roughing' removed the bark and reduced the block to just over the required size. After 'rincing' to clear the central hole, the reels were dried in the kiln ready for finishing. Braithwaites of Staveley and Crook, and Fells of Troutbeck Bridge made nearly all the specialised machinery used in the local bobbin mills. A skilled turner, using a Fell's lathe like **55-65**, might produce 40 reels per minute. With the spindle rotating at 3,000 rpm accidents could, and quite often did happen, as Mr Garside's amputated fingers show in **79-40**.

51-74. Tubular blocking saw by Braithwaite's of Staveley, supplier to Oakbank and Horrax. Ambleside 1967

79-40 Mr E. M. Garside. Retired ex-Horrax (Ambleside) bobbin turner. April 2003

55-65 Finishing lathe – Stott Park. March 1967

60-43 Spark Bridge bobbin mill at closure. October 1983

60-43. Spark Bridge bobbin mill was built in 1850, on the site of the old iron foundry, by Thomas Philipson, whose father had worked in, and later owned, several bobbin mills in the Staveley area. Another branch of the family had an important bobbin mill in Keswick. Thomas married into the Braithwaite (bobbin mill machinery) family and two further generations of Philipsons managed the Spark Bridge mill before selling out in 1965 to Borells, who made bobbins for electrical wire.

23-160. The Howk Bobbin Mill is situated about 500 m from the centre of Caldbeck at the end of a pretty limestone gorge. The Cald Beck fell sufficiently through the gorge to power a very large waterwheel, 42'5" (13.1 m) in diameter and 3' (0.9 m) wide, which was set across the back of the mill. The coppice barn, originally with two floors, has the rectangular pillars typical of one built after 1850. The building on the right was a drying kiln. The mill mostly produced bobbins for the textile industry, but also made tool handles, washing dollies, mole traps, clog soles and other turned goods when the textile industry was going through one of its periodic downturns. The mill was opened in 1857 and worked until 1924; it was originally owned by John Jennings, who leased it to Mr W Helme, the owner of Low Mill (Priests Mill), a corn mill in the village. At its busiest, it employed between 40 and 60 men and boys, working 12 hours a day, six days a week.

23-160 Howk bobbin mill, Caldbeck. May 1986

Brushmaking

Brushmaking was a significant industry in both Kendal and Ulverston, using local coppice wood prepared by mills such as that of John and Moses Simpson of Duddon Bridge, who in 1829 advertised themselves as "brush stock and handle manufacturers".

Rainforth Hodgson was the principal firm in Kendal, operating from their Blackhall works, 69 Stricklandgate, from 1869 and a factory on Sandes Avenue from the 1920s until the late 1960s. Their premises in Stricklandgate were identified by the "Bristling Hog" sign over the door (**9-72**). This model is now in the Kendal Museum of Lakeland Life and Industry, a new version is to be seen over the doorway of 69 Stricklandgate.

In their heyday, Rainforth Hodgson made a very wide range of brushes, from delicate artists' paintbrushes to yard brooms. Their sales records include brushes with unfamiliar uses 'Banister', 'Hat', 'Grate', 'Water' etc. One wall of their outer office in Sandes Avenue, where orders were taken

9-72 The sign of the brush-maker, Blackhall, Kendal. July 1964

9-76 Rainforth Hodgson. Some brush varieties. January 1965

9-90 Boning the chestnut scrubs, Rainforth Hodgson. January 1965

and sales made, was covered with pigeon-holes containing every type of vegetable fibre and animal hair from squirrel tail to pigs' bristle, imported from all over the world. By 1963 however, their output was mainly scrubbing brushes and shippon brooms and they were reduced to two full-time and two part-time brushmakers.

9-90. A horse's thigh-bone was used for this process, which closed the pores of the wood to prevent rot.

In 1931, two Rainforth Hodgson employees set up in competition as Armer & Blamire. Arthur Armer died in 1946, but James Blamire continued working in premises at 13 Lowther St and later in Beezon Road, until he retired in 1979. Mike photographed Jim Blamire making a yard brush at the Lowther St premises in January 1965 as shown in **9-87**, **9-92** and **9-86**.

9-87. The stock for these 'pan-set' or 'pitch-set' brushes was made from ash, sycamore or silver birch, seasoned in the same way as for bobbins.

9-87 Shaping the brush stock, Jim Blamire. January 1965

9-92. Drilling the holes for the filling material (the term 'bristle' was reserved for pig hair). The drill controlled the depth of the holes but the angle, which varied to suit the profile of the brush, was judged by eye.

9-86. A 'knot' of bass fibre was selected and tied with a fine hemp twine known as 'thrim' before dipping the end in hot Stockholm tar (made by destructive

9-92 Boring brush holes. January 1965

distillation of pine wood). After insertion in the hole, the knot was twisted to ensure good adhesion. Jim was able to make a yard brush head in 12 minutes.

9-86 Fixing the 'bristles'. January 1965

Tanning

In the 18th and 19th centuries tanning was an important local industry; most towns had at least one tannery. In the south of the county the extensive coppice woodlands provided the oak bark essential for the tanning process, which involved large volumes of water, so the sites were usually near a river or mill race. Water powered, or in some cases wind or horse powered grinding mills were used to release the tannin from the bark for the lengthy tanning process, which could take up to 15 months. The small local tanneries were later replaced by larger mechanised establishments, as established near Millom, where rotary vats considerably shortened the processing time. An offshoot of the tanning industry was the development of shoemaking in Kendal – K shoes.

9-17 Jack and Young Billy Allonby bark peeling. 1970

9-17. Oak bark is stripped from the coppiced branches in the spring and early summer when rising sap allows the bark to separate easily. The bundles of bark seen in **300-184** were awaiting collection for transport to the traditional tannery of J & FJ Baker & Co, in Colyton, South Devon, which provides an outlet for Furness oak bark to this day.

Bill Hogarth, who coppiced these Rusland woods when coppicing was a dying craft, passed on his enthusiasm and woodland

300-184 Oak bark, Skowbarrow Woods lane, Rusland. 1983

9-27 Bark peelers' hut. Blake Holme Wood, S.E. Windermere shore. January 1995.

skills to others, earning an MBE for his services. After his death in 1999, a trust was set up, running 3-year apprenticeships in coppice skills.

9-27. These low walls and a fireplace on the right are what remains of a building which would have had a tent-like roof of branches supporting a turf covering. Under the leaf litter you might find a stone-flagged floor. This is where the woodsmen used to live during the bark peeling season, sometimes accompanied by their family.

59-33. Rusland's disused tannery, built in the mid 18th century, has now been preserved by the Lake District National Park Authority. The curved projection in the centre of the outer wall housed a horse-gin which powered the bark crushing machinery, rather than using water or wind power. It was a "heavy leather tannery", supplying the leather for such things as boot uppers and soles, harnesses, and strong straps.

59-33 Rusland Tannery. March 1971

59-44 The last remaining tanner's beam. April 1971

59-44. This sandstone hogback or tanner's beam can be seen at Rusland tannery. It would have been used when scraping away the skin and hair after the first stage of treatment of the hides with lime. After washing, the hides were soaked in a series of tannin pits of increasing strength, made from the ground oak bark. The remains of slate and timber lined tan pits have been found inside the eastern end of the building.

120-63. The louvred windows suggest that the upstairs of this building was used by the adjacent tannery which has since been converted into housing. Mill Brow was the main industrial area of Kirkby Lonsdale. A beck running under Market Street emerged

120-63 Tannery building by weighbridge at Mill Brow Head, Kirkby Lonsdale. April 2000

there to drive seven waterwheels before joining the River Lune at the bottom of the steep bank, powering at various times two corn mills, a bark mill to serve two tanneries, a snuff mill, a bone mill, sawmills, a carpet and woollen blanket mill and a print works. The beck was supplied with water from Terry Bank Tarn three miles NNW of the town.

225-11. Early Ordnance Survey maps show two tanneries beside Tom Rudd Beck, a tributary of the River Cocker. They were no doubt supplied with hides by premises in nearby Skinner Street, while on the opposite side of the beck, Little Mill, previously a corn mill, was leased to a tanner for grinding bark from 1763 to 1810.

225-11 Tom Rudd Beck tannery, Cockermouth.

Charcoal

From Medieval times, charcoal was needed for industrial processes, notably as a fuel for metal smelting and as an ingredient in gunpowder. Charcoal production was carried out in the woods on levelled platforms known as pitsteads (**9-68**) which can be seen in many Cumbrian woods. Charcoal is still made in these woods, but in a metal kiln as shown in **9-220**.

9-68 Built-up charcoal pitstead, Rusland.

9-220. To make charcoal, wood needs to be heated in the absence of air. Traditionally, this was achieved by covering a burning stack with green bracken and soil, but the metal kiln achieves the same ends with much less labour. The white steam / smoke shows that the process is not yet complete. Mike participated in several experimental charcoal 'burns' using the traditional methods. The following photos record the progress of one at Ickenthwaite, Rusland, constructed in June 1972 and burned in August. Jack Allonby was the 'collier' in charge.

9-220 Charcoal kiln, Finsthwaite. September 1993

63-17 Ickenthwaite. June 1972

63-17 shows the stack in the early stage of construction round the central 'motty peg'. The thickest timbers are stacked in the centre, where the heat will be greatest.

63-16. The stack is covered with a layer of green bracken (seaves) followed by sieved soil (sammel). In the background you can see the moveable screens to protect the burning

63-62 Jack Allonby and Bill Norris completing the stack. June 1972

63-16 Closing the stead, seaves and sammel. August 1972

stack from the wind, and the traditional charcoal burners' hut where they would stay to monitor the progress of the burn and add more sammel or damp down (say) the stack with water should it show signs of bursting into flames. The process takes about three days, and the stack is then sayed and left to cool down.

63-32. To light the stack, the motty peg is removed and burning charcoal poured down in its place. The hole is then plugged with a sod of turf.

63-32 Stack has just been lit. Last charcoal added by Jack. August 1972

63-74 Day 5. Opening the stack. Did we do well? 8 a.m, 1st September 1972

63-76 Jack Allonby with his charcoal and the saying barrel on its stretcher. 1st September 1972

TEXTILES

Wool

For many centuries sheep have grazed the Cumbrian pastures and fells, and their wool has been spun and woven as a cottage industry. Following the Norman Conquest whole areas of Cumbria were apportioned to one religious house or another, for example Furness Abbey, which generated much of its income by keeping large flocks on their lands and improving the quality of fleeces in order to attract foreign buyers. Hundreds of fleeces would be packed into sacks for export to the Continent. After the Dissolution of the Monasteries, in the mid-1500s, wool went for sale in local market towns and tax changes encouraged the production of cloth here, rather than abroad.

53-3. The wool sacks from this farm were destined for Wool Growers Ltd, a wholesaler in Carnforth.

54-15 Hand-clipping a Swaledale ewe, Caldbeck. June 1988

53-3 Modern shearers at work, Sandgate Farm, Flookburgh. June 1988.

220-47 Woolsacks being taken from Pickles' warehouse, Kendal, to Bradford Wool Market. c.1970

42-26 Roger Ridding Potash kiln, Rusland. April 1972

53-16 Yellow Dyers Greenweed, Lickbarrow, Windermere. May 1970

The rising importance of the woollen industry in the area was not only due to the large numbers of sheep, but also the ready access to clean, soft water and potash soap, which was made locally from burning bracken in potash kilns (**42-26**). It was customary to gather the bracken soon after Michaelmas Day (29th September) while it was still green. After burning, the resulting ash, dissolved in water, was mixed with lime and tallow to produce a soft soap for use in the fulling mills.

53-16. Dyers Greenweed, *Genista tinctoria*, which grew locally, was used to give a yellow dye. Further dyeing with Woad, which was cultivated in other parts of the country, notably in Northumberland on the banks of the Tyne, produced the green colour for which Kendal was famed. Lichens were also used to produce a red dye, popular for cloaks (Little Red Riding Hood).

79-82. This was one of the 18 fulling mills in Grasmere Parish in the 16th century. Here the newly woven and dyed cloth would be beaten with water-driven hammers in soapy water. This caused the woollen fibres to 'felt' or mesh together, giving a thicker, more wind and rain resistant material.

The more remote fulling mills, like this one, fell into ruin as production became concentrated in workshops and factories where mechanical spinning, and later weaving, developed. Other fulling mills were converted into corn mills, bobbin mills etc. In this photo the wheelpit and tailrace are seen in the centre foreground with the mill foundations to the right. A headrace took water from further up Sourmilk Gill, and carried it to the waterwheel in a launder.

53-93. After fulling, which resulted in considerable shrinkage, the cloth needed to be stretched back into shape and dried. Each fulling mill would have its tenter grounds where the material was fixed to frames with copper hooks through the selvages. The place name records the location of tenters on Kendal Fell, tenter grounds being located in positions open to the prevailing winds wherever possible (**53-65**).

53-93 Cloth on tenter hooks, High Tenterfell, Kendal. May 1971

53-65 Tenterbanks at Old Scale, Wythop. June 1980

79-82 High Fulling Mill, Easedale, Grasmere. April 1988

24-249 Millbeck loom sheds, built 1845. Mill from 1776, with jennies. April 1968

24-249. The invention of the spinning jenny in 1764, initially hand-powered, was the first stage in the industrialisation of the production of textiles. The production of the yarn was carried out in workshops or factories, but it was then distributed to

*69-22 Rawes Mill. Woollen mill. Original Mule Shed + Family Cottages.
Hand Jennies in 1828 April 1966*

weavers with looms in their homes. Millbeck mill, Underskiddaw, was spinning wool in 1776 but by 1845 the weaving was also carried on here in 'loom sheds'.

69-22. Originally a fulling mill recorded from 1582, Rawes Mill, Staveley, was rebuilt in 1816 as a woollen mill, powered from the River Gowan. The waterwheel was where the large doorway is in the photo. In 1844 it was advertised to let as a four storey building, 49 ft (15 m) long, 37 ft (11 m) wide, with a steam engine. By 1913 it was one of the many bobbin mills in the Staveley area, until it burned down in 1940.

91-381. The spinning jenny was improved upon by Samuel Crompton's spinning mule, which could be water-powered and have up to 1,320 spindles. Originally designed for cotton spinning, where it produced a fine, strong yarn, it could be used for all types of textiles and was in general use into the early 20th century, and to the present day for niche production of, for example, cashmere.

91-381 Mule at Braithwaite's, Mealbank Mill. 200 spindles. June 1965

80-97. By the late 19th century, woollen mills such as Braithwaite's at Meal Bank, just north of Kendal, were carrying out all the processes of preparing, (**91-375**) spinning (**91-381**) and weaving (**91-383**) on one site. This mill was originally water, but later steam powered; it continued in production until 1965 when the moveable plant was transferred to Farfield Mill near Sedbergh, and the firm continued in business there under a new name - Messrs. Mealbank Woollens Ltd, producing high quality cloths,

80-97 Mealbank Mill. March 1966

91-375 Teazing and carding Swaledale wools for tweeds, Mealbank Mill. May 1965

some of them used by top fashion houses such as Dior and Balenciaga. The Meal Bank site, with 29 houses and a school, was sold by auction in February 1966.

91-383. Dobcross looms were widely used and versatile - with little modification they could be used for textiles ranging from lightweight suitings to heavy blankets. They

91-383 Mealbank Dobcross loom. June 1965

242-5 Howgill Woollen Mill, Sedbergh. July 1981

18-94 Kendal Hosiery Works built 1897. December 1986

could weave with up to 7 shuttles, each with a different colour. This Dobcross loom, transferred from Meal Bank, can still be seen in action at Farfield Mill, Sedbergh.

Woollen goods were not only woven - knitted socks, gloves, caps etc. were made by men, women and children in their own homes. By holding one needle in a wooden 'knitting stick' tucked into a belt or waistband, and the other in the right hand, the left hand was free to do another task.

242-5. Also known as Bland or Blonds Mill, it was driven by water from Blonds Gill, a tributary of the Lune. The woollen yarn spun here was sent out to hand-knitters, and the resulting garments returned for washing, fulling and finishing. Census returns suggest that the mill was no longer operating in 1871.

18-94. By the late 19th century, knitting was also becoming mechanised. In 1878 E.W.Thompson started making hosiery on hand-operated knitting machines in premises on Sandes Avenue and at Stramongate Mill. Later named Kendal Socks, production rose to 8 million pairs per annum before closure in the late 1980s.

The last of Kendal's woollen industries was carpet making, which continued at Goodacre's Castle Mills until 2005.

13-177. Highgate Woollen Mill was at this time part of Goodacres Carpets. According to a Westmorland Gazette report of a major fire during the night of October 31st 1967, 120 people were employed at the Highgate mill, preparing the wool for weaving on the other side of the river at Castle Mills, where 300 were employed.

13-177 The Highgate Mills below Miller Bridge, Kendal. January 1960

Flax and Linen

Flax was widely grown, especially around the fringes of the Lake District, for domestic use until the middle of the 18th century, linen thread sometimes being woven with wool or cotton to give a harder wearing fabric. Sites of flax growing can often be identified by 'lin' in part of the name eg. Lindale, Linthwaite. Later, flax was imported from Ireland and the Baltic states.

119-25 Old retting pond by Howe Farm, above Town End, Grasmere. February 2000

119-25. The stalks of flax or hemp (for ropes) were weighted down with stones and left to soak in purpose-built retting ponds which can often be recognised by their vertical sides and uniform depth of about 2 ft (0.6m). The softer parts rotted after 2-3 weeks and after drying, scotching removed the unwanted material, leaving the fibres to be heckled (combed) to align them ready for spinning.

The necessary softening of the fibres was achieved by a process similar to that for fulling wool, with mechanical hammers and soap made with potash. Bleaching of linen cloth was sometimes carried out in the same premises, using potash soap and urine which was often collected from 'piss-pots' strategically placed outside local ale-houses.

22-55. As spinning became mechanised, flax mills were built, notably at Cockermouth, but also at Ambleside, Holme, Milnthorpe, Penny Bridge and Egremont. Like the cotton mills, they were normally four storey buildings. Rubby Banks mill was used at various times as a corn mill, fulling mill, flax mill, cotton mill and for making hats.

22-147. Fitz Mill was built as a flax mill in 1794 but later used for other textiles, manufacturing woollen goods and spinning carpet yarns. The mill was dual-powered, using 3 waterwheels but also steam power (note the large chimney). By 1900 it was marked on maps as disused and it was demolished about 1980.

22-55 Rubby Banks flax mill, Cockermouth. April 1968

22-147 Fitz Mill, Cockermouth. Note a 4th (garret) floor on both mills - cotton or flax. There was a corn mill just below the flax mill so the tailrace was also a headrace, so it was longer than usual to ensure no back-up. October 1969

22-24 Derwent Mill, Cockermouth, built 1834, 5 floors. May 1976

22-24. Harris's Derwent Mills were constructed in 1834 and expanded over the next 20 years, They were spinning flax to produce embroidery threads in over 200 shades, but also weaving to make linen goods. (**22-25**). Up to 800 people were employed at one time. The premises were converted to shoemaking at the start of WW2 until closure in the early 1990s.

21-198. Henry Birley & Co. built this mill, with its distinctive façade, in 1800; the four storey factory building is behind.

21-198 Birley Mill, Cleator. October 1994

In an 1829 directory they were described as "flax and tow spinners, thread, twine, sailcloth etc. manufacturers". A 100 hp (75kW), 20 ft (6m) diameter waterwheel was commissioned in the 1830s, but the chimney suggests that steam power was also used. In 1938 it became the headquarters of Kangol, who made berets for the armed forces and as fashion items.

22-25 Advert; Harris at Cockernauth

Cotton

Following the invention of water-powered spinning machinery in the latter part of the 18th century, cotton mills were built along a number of Cumbrian rivers. Some were short-lived and quite quickly converted to other uses, such as the cotton mill at Cark, which became a corn mill in 1816 after experimenting with an early Boulton & Watt steam engine to recycle the limited water supply.

Eighty percent of the raw cotton was imported from America, so the cotton famine created by the American Civil War (1861-5), combined with overproduction as the large Lancashire steam-driven mills dominated the market, led to the closure or conversion of many of the local cotton mills, for example the mill at Backbarrow, which was converted into the Blue Works in 1890. Even around Carlisle, which by the mid 1800s had four large spinning mills in the city and others at Dalston, Warwick Bridge and Cummersdale, the cotton famine led to bankruptcy and a change to woollen textiles. Today, only the dyeing and printing of textiles at Cummersdale, on the southern outskirts of Carlisle, survive to remind us of Cumbria's former cotton industry.

60-80. Mrs Hemer was born in 1887 and started work in the Spark Bridge cotton carding mill at the age of 10. Later, she became one of the hundreds of outworkers who used the hanks of yarn spun in the local mills to weave or, in her case, to crochet items such as shawls, table cloths, antimacassars, 'lace' curtains etc.

60-80 Mrs Hemer, Lowick Bridge, Spark Bridge Mill outworker. July 1967.

70-15 Barley Bridge Cotton Mill. 5 windows to left of central stairs, 6 windows to right. January 1973

70-15. Barley Bridge Cotton Mill, Staveley, was part of a cluster of mill buildings on both sides of the River Kent, including a fulling mill, a corn mill, a very early bobbin mill and a woollen mill. The four storey cotton mill, built in 1783, was sold 10 years later, and then bought back again and improved machinery installed. By 1811, however, it was being used as a woollen mill and continued as such intermittently

15-189 Hartley's Low Mill, Ulverston. February 1989

until 1906, when it was leased, and later bought, by a firm making photographic paper – Kentmere Ltd. In 2008 the photo paper business was taken over by Harman Technology of Knutsford, leaving Kentmere as a packaging manufacturer.

15-189. This, the largest and most successful of the Ulverston cotton mills, built on a medieval iron working site in the late 18th century, was initially water-powered from Lund Beck but used steam from about 1830. By 1888 it was described as "defunct" and was converted into a tannery by Randall & Porter, continuing until 1971.

11-142 Otterburn Mill & cottages. Warwick Bridge. Only 4 floors (a garret) in this view. February 1974

11-142. Also known as Langthwaite, this cotton mill was completed by the Ferguson brothers in 1792, but had to be rebuilt in 1793 following a fire. They continued until 1809, when the mill was leased to Peter Dixon & Sons, who built a new wing and cottages, as well as a reservoir. When their new mill in Carlisle was completed in 1836 (**20-5**), the firm tried unsuccessfully to dispose of the Langthwaite lease and in 1872 were declared bankrupt. However, they re-emerged as a limited company and used Langthwaite as a dye and bleach works.

20-5. Built in 1835-36 for Peter Dixon, Shaddon Mill was designed by Richard Tattersall as a steam-powered cotton

20-5 Shaddon Mill, Carlisle, built 1836. 1971

spinning mill. The main mill building is 7 storeys high by 22 bays and was the largest cotton mill in England at the time. Attached at the west end was a two storey boiler house, and between it and the main mill was the engine house. The chimney, known locally as Dixon's chimney, was originally 320 ft (97.5 m) high from foundations to top and was one of the highest chimneys in the world. Built by local firm Richard Wright, it is octagonal, built of brick with sandstone quoins. After a lightning strike in 1931, 50 ft (15 m) was removed from the top, leaving it at 270 ft.

In the 1880s both Langthwaite and Shaddon became woollen mills. Shaddon Mill is now converted into flats, but the weaving sheds behind the mill are still used to produce Linton Tweed.

20-149. Prior to 1828 the Holme Head site was used by Messrs Carrick and Johnston, cotton spinners, but was then rented by Joseph Ferguson, the founder of the firm that subsequently developed it into a complete cotton processing site with spinning, weaving, dyeing, printing and finishing, with alterations to allow new processes and machinery.

He had a specific treatment called 'beetling' (similar to fulling of woollens) which gave the finished cotton cloth a soft feel.

The weir, on the River Caldew, was rebuilt in 1865 after severe flood damage in 1862. The building to the right was also severely damaged in the flood and was rebuilt at the same time. It was used for 'beetling'. The other building was the main office block dating from 1837.

The site eventually closed in 1997 and the buildings have now been converted to housing.

20-149 Weir, Holme Head Mills, Carlisle. October 1987

15-118 Holme Head Works. October 1987

BACKBARROW BLUE WORKS

The Lancashire Ultramarine Company was set up in 1890, making synthetic ultramarine blue pigment in the former Ainsworth's cotton mill – a cheap replacement for powdered lapis lazuli which had been used as a pigment since Neolithic times. The waterwheel of the cotton mill was replaced by a Gilkes turbine.

The Backbarrow blue works was commonly referred to as the "Dolly Blue factory", although the cartons of laundry whitener it produced were not sold under that particular brand name.

91-430 Backbarrow Dolly Blue – kilns in North Mill. August 1981

91-436 Dolly Blue kiln No. 7. 1981

91-430. The raw materials for making ultramarine blue included sulphur, imported from Sicily, charcoal, bones, china clay, sodium carbonate and pitch. These ingredients were ground in a ball mill to form a greyish-brown powder and then heated for three days in crucibles (seen here stacked against the wall on the left) in one of the kilns. Once full, the kiln doors were blocked up and steel guillotine doors closed over them, balanced by weights over pulleys. Large exhaust gas and smoke hoods sat over the kiln tops linking them with the chimney.

91-436 shows the crucibles stacked in an opened kiln. At this stage the yellow colour of the sulphur predominates. The kilns were originally coal-fired, but later converted to L.P.G. The process produced quantities of sulphur dioxide fumes which were dispersed from the tall chimney seen in **125-22**. The resulting solid blue material had to be broken up and washed to remove impurities, which were discharged into the river (**91-429**).

91-429 Sludge remover. August 1981

125-22 Backbarrow. January 1963

125-22. Backbarrow Blue Works from the Iron Works site under the smoggy conditions that will be remembered by those who used the A590 through this industrial village before the bypass was built in the mid-1960s. After passing between the Blue Mill buildings, the busy main road crossed the narrow bridge over the river and then passed between the iron furnace stack and the ore and coke storage sheds.

91-419 and **19-124**. Further grinding, washing and drying meant that the blue powder permeated the building and covered the workers. There was no extraction system, and the blue dust in the air and on the windows made the interior of the mill dark and hazardous.

91-419 Backbarrow Blue Mills c. 1975

19-124 "Dolly Blue" kiln worker (Reckitts). 1971

91-398. Lancahire Ultramarine Co. wagon 1971

91-441 Dolly Blue Mill load delivered by 'RED'!

The final product was sold for use in artists' materials, cosmetics, printing ink, paint, paper manufacture and in small cartons for "whitening" laundry, much of it going overseas.

91-398. The original Lancashire Ultramarine Company was taken over by Reckitts of Hull in 1928. The factory closed in 1982 when it became clear that it could not meet modern health and safety and environmental standards. The main buildings have been converted into a hotel and leisure club; timeshare apartments and a motor museum have been added on the site. A few blue stains remain.

91-447 Converting the blue mills into a hotel and leisure club. August 1984

TRANSPORT

Roads

Since Neolithic times and the need to transport the stone axes made in the central fells, through to the present day, transport has always been important to people and their associated industry.

In 1555 legislation was introduced to make each parish responsible for maintaining the roads through its area by using the unpaid labour of the parishioners. This was not very successful, especially in those parishes which had major highways or bridges largely used by traffic from elsewhere. It led to the introduction of turnpike roads controlled by trusts, which levied a charge on all users, the proceeds being used to maintain the roads. The first turnpike trust in Cumbria was at Whitehaven in 1739, its roads principally constructed to ease the movement of coal to the harbour.

Cumbria was an important area in the droving trade moving cattle and sheep from Scotland to the markets in the south of the country. These herds and flocks generally followed specific routes which became known as drove roads. They tended to follow open country avoiding towns, and were wide to allow the animals to graze as they travelled and also to prevent too much damage to the surface. Similar roads were developed during the enclosure period to allow access to the newly enclosed land and the wastes beyond. The practice of droving animals long distances to market was all but extinguished by the advent of the railways.

31-12. Although Mike labelled this as a drove road, and it does have the look of a drove road, this is an enclosure road. Until the 17th century, a large proportion of the land in the country was classed as common land or, in the uplands, waste, and people of

31-12 Drove road on Gilderdale Forest, west of Alston. January 1989

the village or manor were free to graze their animals on the land. From the mid 18th century there was a move to enclose these wastes and improve the land for grazing. To allow access to these new fields and to the unenclosed hills beyond, enclosure roads were usually laid out straight at a set width of 60 ft (18 m), reducing to 30 ft in the mid 19th century.

31-44. Until the turnpike roads were constructed, wheeled traffic was rare in the Lake District. People travelled on horseback, and goods were transported by trains of packhorses. More than 20 teams of packhorses linked Kendal with the main Cumbrian towns and further afield when trade was at its height. Many packhorse routes have since been converted to roads but those of the central fells went over passes such as Nan Bield and Stake Pass, which are now only used by walkers. They may be recognised by the zigzag tracks on the steeper gradients, and the narrow packhorse bridges with little or no parapet.

As with the drovers, accommodation was needed for men and horses at the end of each day's travel of about 15 miles. The packhorse inn would have had a pulley system to lift the saddles (**18-127**) and their loads, which could weigh over 200 lbs (90 kg), from the horses' backs, avoiding the need for unpacking the goods each night.

18-127 Pack saddle, Eskdale. September 1986

31-44 Mosedale bridge, Wasdale. October 1965.

5-8 Dunmail Raise. January 1959.

5-8. A turnpike trust set up in 1762 included a highway from Keswick to Kendal over Dunmail Raise, the lowest and most frequented of the Lakeland passes. Since this photo was taken in 1959, the road has been greatly widened on the south side and a short

66-118 Roads (3), rail and river at Lune Gorge and Tebay Roman fort. August 1986

section of dual carriageway added at the summit. The north side, however, remains largely unaltered from turnpike days and can catch the motorist unawares, although repairs and some modifications were made in the wake of 2015's storm damage, which closed the road for several months.

66-118. The Lune Gorge has provided a thoroughfare for many centuries. The Romans built a fort at Low Borrow Bridge (upper left of the photo). They obviously thought the route important enough to be protected by a garrison of 500 infantrymen. The original route of the 1762 Kendal – Brough turnpike, later the A685, was destroyed by the construction of the M6. Its replacement was built higher up the valley side and now sweeps gracefully over motorway, railway and river to join the former route in the foreground, where the original turnpike bridge can also be seen.

Railways

The earliest known use of rails in Britain was by the German miners in Elizabethan times, in the mines of the Caldbeck Fells. The use of railways to transport goods wagons pulled by horses or gravity was further developed in the coal mining areas. The first public steam powered railway to open in Cumbria was the Newcastle to Carlisle railway in 1836. A large network of lines developed during the 19th century, especially in the west of the county, linking the various iron and coal mines to the ports and iron works. The west coast main railway line, which was opened in 1846, used the route through the Lune Gorge (**66-118**) in preference to the other options of a coastal route via West Cumberland, or a tunnel from the head of Longsleddale to Mardale.

19-111 Milnthorpe (Bela) Viaduct. Arches show that vessels still expected. August 1966

66-93 Oliver Cromwell departing Windermere Station. April 1968

19-111. What was known as the Kendal branch of the Furness Railway was opened in 1876 to link the Furness Railway at Arnside with the London and North Western Railway at Hincaster Junction, south of Oxenholme. It provided the Furness Railway with the means of providing a passenger service between Grange and Kendal. The chief engineering requirement was the crossing of the River Bela where it entered the estuary of the Kent. Unfortunately, the landowner stipulated that the viaduct should be removed once it was no longer required for railway purposes and demolition was carried out in 1966, after that section of the line had ceased to be used in 1963.

66-93. The Kendal to Windermere Railway opened in 1847 as a double track main line with trains to various destinations, including London Euston. At Windermere, extensive coach sidings were built to accommodate excursion trains – as many as 17 could arrive on a Sunday. By the 1960s, however, traffic had declined and the goods yard closed in 1969. In 1973 the railway was reduced to a single track, the signal box closed and in the early 1980s the station buildings were sold and converted into a Booths supermarket, the warehouses and goods yard providing a site for Lakeland Limited.

On this occasion, April 20th 1968, Britannia Class engine 70013, Oliver Cromwell, had brought an excursion train from Fleetwood and was departing for Morecambe. There is another steam engine in the station.

66-47 Muncaster Mill Bread Van - La'al Ratty rolling stock. June 1996

66-48 Muncaster Mill and La'al Ratty. June 1989

66-47 (previous page) and **66-48**. The Ravenglass and Eskdale Railway opened in 1875 as a 3 ft (914 mm) gauge line to carry iron ore from several small mines in Eskdale. In spite of the addition of passenger traffic in 1876, and granite freight from 1905, the company was always in financial difficulty and the railway closed in 1913. In 1915 it was taken over by Narrow Gauge Railways Ltd and the track re-laid as 15 inch (381 mm) gauge. The early scale model locomotives, designed by W.J. Bassett-Lowke, were intended for use on seaside promenades or the gardens of stately homes and struggled with the Eskdale gradients, sometimes requiring the passengers to get out and walk. However, thanks to some wealthy steam enthusiasts and the provision of additional steam and diesel locomotives, the line stayed open. A 2.5 mile section of the line from Ravenglass was, in 1929, also equipped with standard gauge (4ft 8 1/2) track laid astride the 15" rails in connection with a rock crushing plant at Murthwaite, designed to relieve unemployment in the district and provide extra revenue for the railway. Quarried rock was brought by the narrow gauge trains from Beckfoot, discharged for processing and then carried by standard gauge wagons to Ravenglass for onward conveyance by the LMSR, much of it being used as railway ballast. The Murthwaite plant closed in 1953.

In 1960 the Ravenglass and Eskdale Railway Preservation Society raised the money to buy the line and a company was set up to run the railway. In 1964 it returned the first operating profit in 70 years, and has flourished since then as a tourist attraction. The engine in **66-48** is the Northern Rock, built at Ravenglass in 1976.

Water transport

The use of inland water transport in Cumbria has been limited by the lack of navigable rivers and terrain unsuitable for canal building. The Lancaster Canal terminated at Kendal and the canals at Ulverston and Carlisle were short in length and in time span. The larger lakes such as Windermere, Ullswater, Derwentwater and Coniston Water did provide some passenger transport and the conveyance of materials such as iron and copper ores, slate, stone and timber. Apart from the ferry across the middle of Windermere, which continues to provide a useful link for local people, Cumbrian lake craft are now devoted to the leisure and tourism industries.

5-107 Busy lake in August 1991.

5-107. This photo illustrates the conflicting interests which led to the implementation of a speed limit of 10 nautical mph on Windermere from March 2005. (Note the capsized boat, apparently in the path of the speedboat and waterskier). Between 1977 and 1991 there had been a 300% increase in the number of speedboats on the lake and on an average day that could mean over 350 such boats. A public inquiry supported the National Park Authority's call for a speed limit, which was initially rejected by the government, but confirmed after the Authority sought a Judicial Review.

Coastal waters and estuaries, by contrast, were extensively used to transport raw materials and finished products, leading to the development of boat and ship building industries from the Solway to Morecambe Bay, but particularly in Barrow, where submarine construction has now largely taken over from the building of surface vessels.

7-81 Whitehaven harbour. July 1967

7-81. The development of Whitehaven harbour was started in 1634 by Sir Christopher Lowther, who built a stone quay (The Old Quay) to allow coal to be exported, mainly to Ireland. Over time more quays were added, including the Sugar Tongue Quay to allow the unloading of sugar from the West Indies. This trade with the West Indies and the coal exports made Whitehaven the country's second largest port after London in the 18th century.

The last commercial development was Queen's Dock, built in the 1870s. The dock was originally used for exporting coal, but in its final phase it was used by Marchon Chemicals to import calcium phosphate from Africa to make detergents. The conveyor and silos can be seen in this photo.

7-98. Whitehaven did not have sufficient depth of water to allow modern shipping to enter the port, so Marchon used their own ships to bring calcium phosphate from larger ships anchored off-shore into the port for unloading.

7-38 Marchon incline, Whitehaven. May 1980

7-98 Phosphate handling, Whitehaven. 1979

7-38. Originally built in 1881 by the Earl of Lonsdale's Whitehaven Colliery Co. to bring coal from Croft Pit to the Furness Railway, it had a number of different names, including Corkickle Brake Incline and Croft Pit Incline. The incline was altered in 1904 to allow it to cope with increased traffic from the new Ladysmith Colliery. It stopped moving coal in 1932 and lay idle until 1955 when the Marchon chemical works started to use it to move chemicals to and from its factory. It was last used on 4th November 1986, when it was the last ropeworked incline in the UK.

39-123. Workington harbour lies at the mouth of the River Derwent. It started to be developed in the mid 18th Century with the export of coal. The port developed with increasing trade with the Merchants' Quay and the South Quay built either side of a branch of the Derwent called the South Gut. The Lonsdale dock was opened in 1865 and the breakwater was built in 1873. The

39-123 Bucket dredger at Workington dock. March 1963

Lonsdale dock was rebuilt between 1923 and 1927 to give a bigger dock with a wider and easier entrance and was renamed the Prince of Wales Dock. Originally the port was owned by the Earl of Lonsdale but was taken over by the Workington Harbour and Dock Board by an Act of Parliament in 1906. As the export of coal decreased the port's main role was the import of manganese ore used in steelmaking and the export of iron and steel products, especially rails. In 1975 it was sold by the steel company to Cumbria County Council for £1.

The Harbour has always suffered from silting due to both the river and movement of sediments in the Solway and dredging has always been needed. This is the bucket dredger Concur built in 1949 by Fleming and Ferguson of Paisley at the Phoenix yard on the Clyde for the United Steel Company, Workington. It was sold in 1959 to the Workington Harbour and Dock Board and then in 1972 to Societa Anonima Italiana Lavori Edili Marittimi, Palermo Italy. She was a single screw steamer with three cylinders, 165 feet long by 38 feet breadth.

Workington is still a working dock and still requires regular dredging which is now carried out by specialist contractors.

66-270. Boat and shipbuilding was already well established in Barrow in 1871, when James Ramsden started the Iron Shipbuilding Co. This became the Barrow Shipbuilding Co. In 1897 it was bought by Vickers and Co. and was called the Naval Construction and Armament Co. It has had a number of other names during its life.

The yard has, over the years, built liners, commercial ships, oil tankers and naval ships, including aircraft carriers. In the background of **66-271** three naval vessels can be seen. The first of very many submarines was built there in 1886 and the yard has built nearly all of the Royal Navy's nuclear powered submarine fleet. These are now built in the Devonshire Dock Hall, a 250 m long, 51 m high building.

66-271 and **19-167**. One of the last passenger ships built at Barrow was the SS. Oriana for the Orient Steam Navigation Co., for use on the Britain to Australia route. After the Orient Co was taken over by P&O, she was used for cruising, mainly from Sydney. In 1986 she was sold for use as a floating hotel in Japan, and later, China. After suffering damage in a storm in 2004, she was eventually broken up.

19-167 Busy docks, Barrow, dredger and Manx ferry towed in. September 1960

66-270 Midwinter sunrise on Vickers at Barrow. January 1980

66-271 'Oriana' fitting-out, Barrow. 1959

Air transport

Commercial aviation has not featured prominently in Cumbria. In the nineteenth century pleasure balloon flights occurred from various towns such as Carlisle and Kendal which had gasworks to provide the gas. Early in the 20th century Vickers won a government contract to build airships at their Barrow shipyard. The first ship, nicknamed the Mayfly, was not successful, but later, working airships were built until the contract was moved to the Isle of Wight.

Seaplane manufacture at Windermere started as early as 1911 when a local boat builder helped to construct the first British plane to take off from, and land on water, and continued to provide reconnaissance planes for the Royal Navy in WW1. The Second World War saw the return of seaplane manufacture at the lake.

Also during WW2 the Air Force built 11 airfields in Cumbria which were used for training, aircraft storage, and coastal protection. After the war two of these airfields, Walney and Carlisle, tried unsuccessfully to develop commercial passenger flights.

66-314. In July 1990 the world's last airworthy Short Sunderland flying boat visited Windermere. Thirty five Short Sunderlands were built at White Cross Bay, north of Troutbeck Bridge, between 1942 and 1945; many more were repaired or refurbished. Shorts had set up a factory and assembly line there as a site less vulnerable to German bombing than their main production facility at Rochester in Kent. The RAF used the planes for reconnaissance, rescue and, increasingly, for anti-submarine bombing and dropping depth charges. After the war some Sunderlands continued in military service in the Far East and in New Zealand until 1967, but others like this 'Islander' were converted for civil use.

66-314 Port quarter view of 'Islander' flying boat. 6 July 1990

INDEX

Adit, 8, 10
Aerial ropeway, 5, 8, 9
Agricultural machinery, 53, 60
Ainsworth's cotton mill, 107
Air transport, 122
Aircraft carrier, 120
Airship, 122
Alder, 78, 80
Allonby, Jack, 86, 89, 90-92
Allonby, Young Billy, 86
Alston, 111
Ambleside, 3, 56, 81, 100
American Civil War, 103
Ammonia, 44
Anglers Crag, 21
Annie Lowther Pit, 24-25, 26, 27, 31
Archimedean screw turbine, 60
Armer, Arthur, 84
Arnold Pit, 24, 31
Arnside, 115
Ash (tree), 80, 84
Askam, 23
Atomic Weapons Research Establishment, 12
Backbarrow Blue Works, 107-110
Backbarrow Cotton Mill, 103
Backbarrow Iron Co, 33
Backbarrow Iron Furnace, 18, 22, 33-40, 108
Baines, E., 36
Baines, Tommy, 36, 37
Ball mill, 72, 107
Balmoral Castle, 60
Barepot Ironworks, 40
Bark, 86-88
Bark mill, 88
Bark peelers' hut, 87
Barley, 62, 63, 67, 68
Barley Bridge, 79, 104
Barratt, John, 24
Barrel, 63, 72, 76, 92
Barrow (in-Furness), 23, 65, 117, 120-121, 122
Barrow Haematite Iron & Steel Co, 33
Barrow Shipbuilding Co, 120
Barytes, 1, 8-9, 68
Basket making, 77-78
Bass fibre, 85
Bassett-Lowke, W.J., 116
Beam engine, 27-28
Beckermet, 2
Beckfoot, 116
Bedstone, 63
Beer, 67-70
Beetling, 106
Bellows, 21-22, 34
Besom, 75-76
Bessemer converter, 23, 40, 41, 45-48
Birch, 75-76, 80, 84
Birley Mill, 102
Biscuit, 66
Blackhall, 83
Blake Holme, 87
Blamire, James, 84-85
Blanket, 63, 88, 98
Blanket bog, 18
Blast furnace, 22, 33-44, 53
Bleaching, 100, 105
Blocking saw, 81
Bloom, 21, 22, 33, 40, 49
Bloomery, 21, 33, 75
Bloomsmithy, 21-22
Blue works, 103, 107-110
Bobbin, 61, 79-82
Bobbin mill, 57, 58, 59, 79-83, 95, 97, 104
Bone mill, 88
Bones, 107
Boning, 84
Bool, 77
Booth, Fred, 34, 36, 38
Booth's supermarket, 115
Borell's, 82
Boring, 81
Borrowdale, 1, 7, 22
Borwick Rails, 31
Bosh, 41, 42
Bothel, 16-17
Bottom-slicing, 25
Boulton & Watt, 103
Bracken, 89, 90, 94
Braithwaite, 9
Braithwaite's, engineers, 81, 82,
Braithwaite's woollen mill, 97
Brew, R., 78
Breweries, 68-70
Brewery Arts Centre, 70
Brewing, 67-70
Bridge loft, 33
Bristle, 84-85
Bronze Age, 1
Brough, 114
Brushmaking, 83-85
Burlington Stone Co, 3
Cadger, 65
Caine, Nathaniel, 24
Calcium carbonate, 16
Calcium hydroxide, 16
Calcium oxide, 16
Calcium phosphate, 118
Caldbeck, 82-83, 93
Caldbeck Brewery, 69
Caldbeck Fells, 11, 114
Caldewgate, Carlisle, 66
Campaign, 34
CAMRA, 67
Canal, 117
Canal Head, Kendal, 60, 71
Canary, 12
Canvas belt, 80
Carbon, 22, 23, 34, 47
Carbon dioxide, 16, 22, 47
Carbon monoxide, 12, 41, 47
Carding, 79, 98, 103
Carel steam engine, 66
Cark cotton mill, 103
Carlisle, 18, 54-55, 66, 67-68, 103, 105, 106, 114, 117, 122
Carlisle District State Management Scheme, 67-68
Carnforth, 93
Carpet making, 88, 99, 100

Carr, Jonathan Dodgson, 66
Carr's Water Biscuits, 66
Carrick & Johnston, 106
Carron Steel works, 76
Cartmel, 56
Cartmel Fell, 75
Cashmere, 97.
Cast iron, 22, 23, 33, 34, 43, 53-56, 57, 59
Castle Mills, Kendal, 99
Castlegate, Penrith, 53
Caudale Moor, 3
Cementation process, 23
Central Control Board (Liquor Traffic), 67, 68
Chalcopyrite, 10
Chapel Bank Colliery, 15
Charcoal, 18, 21, 22, 23, 33, 34, 75, 89, 91, 92, 107
Charcoal burners' hut, 91
Charcoal making, 89-92
Chestnut, 84
Chimney, 14, 15, 27, 33, 70, 100, 103, 105, 107
China clay, 107
Cinders, 34
Clampitt, George, 30
Cleator, 102
Clipping, 93
Clog (footwear), 78, 82
Clog (slate), 4, 5, 6
Coal, 1, 12, 14-17, 18, 44, 107, 111, 114, 118, 119
Coal gas, 44
Cock & Dolphin, 70
Cockermouth, 62, 69, 88, 100-103
Cogging mill, 40, 49, 50
Coke, 23, 34, 41, 44, 53
Coke oven, 44
Coledale, 8-9
Collier (charcoal maker), 89
Concrete, 26, 27, 33,
Concur, 120
Coniston, 4-5, 60, 68, 117
Coniston Copper mines, 1, 24
Coopering, 76
Copper, 1, 10, 12, 24, 117
Coppice wood, 75-83, 86

Coppicing, 75
Corkickle Brake Incline, 119
Corn mill, 57, 58, 59, 61-66, 72, 82, 88, 95, 100, 101, 103, 104
Cotton, 97, 100, 101, 103-106
Cotton famine 103
Cotton mill, 79, 100, 103-106, 107
Cowans Sheldon, 12, 54
Cowper stove, 41, 42-44
Cracking (mill stone), 64-65
Crane, 6, 31, 37, 41, 47, 49, 52, 54
Croft Pit, 119
Crompton, Samuel, 97
Crook, 81
Crossfield, Stephen, 33
Crosthwaite Corn Mill, 63, 65
Crucible, 23, 107
Cumbria Wildlife Trust, 20
Cummersdale, 103
Cupola, 33
Dalston, 103
Davies, R. B., 29
Derby grit, 65
Derwent Hematite Iron Co, 41
Derwent Iron Works, 41
Derwent Mill, 102
Derwentwater, 117
Detergent, 118
Devonshire Dock Hall, 120
Dickinson, Bob, 37
Distington Engineering, 40
Dixon, Peter, 105
Dobcross loom, 98-99
Dock, 118-120
Dolly Blue, 107, 109, 110
Door knob, 79
Dredger, 119-120
Drilling, 30, 85
Drought, 80
Drove road, 111
Drum, 80
Drum house, 4
Drying house, 61
Drying kiln, 18, 62-63, 81, 82
Drying shed, 79-82

Duddon Bridge, 83
Duddon Estuary, 24
Duke of Cumberland Inn, 70
Duke of Devonshire, 24
Dunmail Raise, 113
Dunnerdale, 76
Dye, 94
Dyeing, 94, 103, 105
Dyer's Greenweed, 94
Dynamo, 59
Eamont Bridge, 71
Earl of Derwentwater, 13
Earl of Lonsdale, 24, 119, 120
Easedale, 95
Egremont, 21, 100
Ehenside Tarn, 2
Electric arc furnace, 23, 40, 41, 49
Elizabethan, 1, 10, 114
Elterwater, 5-6
Embroidery thread, 102
Enclosure road, 111-112
English Heritage, 80
Ennerdale, 21
Ennerdale granite, 63
Eskdale, 20, 78, 112, 116
Eskdale granite, 63, 116
Explosive, 8, 10, 12
Fairbanks, John, 65
Farfield Mill, 97-98
Fault (geological), 1
Fawcett, Jim, 28
Fell's (engineering), 81
Fenders, 75-76
Ferguson, Joseph, 106
Ferry, 117, 120
Finery hearth, 22
Finishing (rails), 49-52
Finishing (wood turning), 81-82
Finsthwaite, 80, 81, 89
Fire crane, 53
Fitz Mill, 100-101
Flax, 100-103
Flax mill, 62, 100-103
Fleece, 93
Flookburgh, 93
Florence Mine, 21

Flux, 17, 34, 41
Flying boat, 122
Force Crag Mine, 8-9
Forge, 22
Foulshaw, 18-20
Foundry, 23, 25, 27, 53-56, 82
Francis turbine, 59
French burr, 63, 64
Fulling mill, 57, 61, 80, 94-95, 97, 100, 104
Furness Abbey, 21, 93
Furness Railway, 115, 119
Furrows, 63, 65
Galena, 10, 11
Garside, Mr E.M., 81
Gas scrubbing plant, 44
Gasworks, 122
Gawith, Hoggarth & Co, 71, 72
Gilbert Gilkes & Gordon (Gilkes), 53, 60, 107
Gilderdale Forest, 111
Glaramara, 2
Goat (Gote) Mill, Cockermouth, 57, 62
Goldscope Mine, 10
Goodacres, 99
Grange (over-sands), 115
Graphite, 1
Grasmere, 95, 100
Great spurwheel, 65
Greenside Mine, 11-12,
Greenwich Hospital, 13
Gretna, 67
Grizebeck, 67
Gunpowder, 60, 76, 89
Hadrian's Wall, 1
Haematite, 21, 24-32, 41
Haig Pit, 1, 14-15
Hair, 84-85
Harbour, 15, 31, 111, 118-119
Hardendale, 17
Harris, Jonathan, 62, 103
Harrison Ainslie & Co, 39
Hartley, William, 78
Hartley's Cotton Mill, 104
Hartleys Brewery, 70
Hartsop, 12-13

Hat making, 100
Haulage jack, 30
Haverthwaite, 18, 60
Hawkshead Hill, 57-58
Hayeswater Gill, 12
Hazel, 76, 77
Headrace, 13, 95, 101
Headstock, 27, 28
Heckling, 100
Helme, W., 82
Helsington Laithes, 71-74
Hemer, Mrs, 103
Hemp, 85, 100
Henry Birley & Co, 102-103
High Dam, 80
High Fulling Mill, 95
High Hall Garth, 53
High Tenterfell, 95
Highgate Brewery, 70
Highgate Woollen Mill, 99
Hincaster Junction, 115
Hodbarrow Mines, 24-32
Hodbarrow Mining Co, 24
Hogarth, Bill, 86
Holme, 100
Holme Head Mill, 106
Honister Slate Quarry, 4
Horrax, 81
Horse gin, 15, 87
Hosiery, 99
Howe Farm, Townend, 100
Howgill Woollen Mill (Bland Mill), 99
Howk Bobbin Mill, 82-83
Hudson Scott Co, 66
Hurdles, 75-76
Hush, 10, 11
Hydro-electric power, 59-60
Ickenthwaite, 89, 90
Illingworths, 71, 72
Incline, 4, 8, 118-119
Ingot, 22, 40, 47-49
Iron, 21-56, 105, 114
Iron furnace, 18, 21, 33-44, 108
Iron ore, 21, 24-32, 33-35, 41, 116, 117
Iron Shipbuilding Co, 120

Ironworks, 23, 25, 33-44, 108, 114
Islander, 122
J & FJ Baker & Co, 86
Jane Pit, 15
Jennings Brewery, 69
Jennings, John, 82
Jigger tray, 73
Jumper (mining), 30
Kangol, 103
Kendal, 53, 54, 56, 60, 70, 71, 83, 94, 95, 112, 113, 115, 117, 122
Kendal Green, 94
Keswick, 60, 82, 113
Kidney ore, 21
Kiln (Backbarrow blue works), 107-109
Kiln (brewing), 67, 68
Kiln (charcoal making), 89
Kiln (corn drying), 18, 62-63
Kiln (lime), 16-17, 18
Kiln shed, 61
Kiln shovel, 63
Kiln tile, 62-63
Kirkby Lonsdale, 88
Kirkoswald Corn Mill, 59
Kirksanton Corn Mill, 63
Knitting, knitting stick, 99
La'al Ratty (Ravenglass & Eskdale Railway), 115-116
Ladysmith Colliery, 119
Lake District National Park Authority, 87, 117
Lakeland Ltd, 115
Lakeside and Haverthwaite railway, 34
Lancashire Ultramarine Co, 107, 109
Lancaster Canal, 117
Langdale Pikes, 2
Langstrath, 22
Langthwaite Mill, 104
Lantern wheel, 65
Lapis lazuli, 107
Laporte Chemicals Ltd, 8
Lat-axe, 77
Lathe, 81-82
Launder, 12, 95
Laundry whitener, 107, 110

Lazonby sandstone, 63
Lead, 1, 8, 10-14
Leather, 78, 86-7
Level (mining), 8, 10, 12, 27, 30
Lewis, Arnold, 12
Lichen, 94
Liddle, George, 13
Lighthouse, 27
Lime, 16, 88, 94
Lime coppice, 75
Limestone, 1, 16-17, 21, 24, 26, 27, 34-35, 41, 72
Lindale, 56, 100
Line shafting, 80
Linen, 100-103
Linton Tweed, 105
Little Langdale, 53
Little Mill, Cockermouth, 88
Little Salkeld Corn Mill, 64
LMS railway, 116
Locomotive, 12, 31, 116
Logwood mill, 62
London and North Western Railway, 115
London Lead Co, 13
Longsleddale, 114
Lonsdale dock, 119
Lonsdale foundry, 56
Loom, 97, 98, 99
Loom shed, 96-97
Lorton, 69
Lound foundry, 54
Low Borrow Bridge, 114
Low Gote (or Goat) Mill, 57, 62
Low Hartsop Mining Co, 12
Low Mill, Caldbeck, 82
Lowca, 44
Lowick Bridge, 75, 103
Lowther Street, Kendal, 71, 84-85
Lowther (family), 1, 118
Lowwood, 18, 60
Machell, John, 33
Malthouse, 67, 68
Malting, 67
Manganese, 34, 120
Manganese dioxide, 2

Marble, 72
Marchon, 118, 119
Mardale, 114
Mare (bench), 77
Marne Valley, 63
Marshall, Dr John, 22
Marstons (brewers), 69
Martindale, J., 76
Maryport, 3, 23, 68, 71
Mash tun, 67
Mawson, Thomas, 62
Mayfly, 122
McVities, 66
Meal Bank, 71, 97-98
Mealbank Mill, 97-98
Mealbank Woollens Ltd, 97
Medieval, 1, 75, 105
Metal Box Co, 66
Methane, 12
Michaelmas Day, 94
Middleton, William, 56
Mill Brow, 88
Mill gears, 64-65
Millbeck Mill, 96
Milling, 61-66, 82
Millom, 23, 24-32, 62
Millom Ironworks, 25
Millstone, 63-65
Milnthorpe, 100, 114
Mine pumping engine, 25, 27-28
Mine tipping truck, 31
Miner, 1, 10, 12, 15, 24, 29-30, 78, 114
Mining, 1, 8-15, 24-32, 57
Moorbank Pit, 28-30
Morecambe, 115
Morecambe Bay, 18, 117
Mosedale, 112
Moss Bay Ironworks, Workington, 40
Motty peg, 90, 91
Mule shed, 96
Muncaster Mill, 64, 65, 115-116
Murthwaite, 116
Myers Head Mine, 12-13
Nan Bield, 112

Narrow Gauge Railways Ltd, 116
National Coal Board, 52
National Grid, 60
National Trust, 9
Natland foundry, 56
Naval vessels, 120
Nelson, Les, 30
Nenthead, 1, 13-14
Nenthead & Tynedale Lead and Zinc Co, 14
Neolithic, 1, 2, 107, 111
New Brewery, 68
Newby Bridge Corn Mill, 65
Newcastle to Carlisle Railway, 114
Newcomen engine, 15
Newland Furnace, 39
Newlands, 10
Norris, Bill, 90
Northern Rock locomotive, 116
O'Brien, Jimmy, 30
Oak, 75, 76-77, 80, 86
Oakbank Mill, 79, 80, 81
Old Brewery, 68
Old Scale, Wythop, 95
Oliver Cromwell locomotive, 115
Open-hearth furnace, 23
Operation Orpheus, 12
Ore, 9-13, 21-22, 24-32
Ore bogie, 29, 30
Orient Steam Navigation Co, 120
Otterburn Mill, 105
Outworker, 103
Oxenholme, 115
Pack saddle, 112
Packhorse, 71, 112
Packhorse bridge, 112
Paper mill, 57
Patterdale, 3, 11, 12
Paxton's Mill, 79
Peat, 18-20
Peat barrow, 18-19
Peat hut, 20
Pelton wheel, 59
Pencil, 1
Pennines, 1, 13, 21, 63

Penny Bridge, 100
Penrith, 53
Pestle & mortar, 72
Philipson, Thomas, 82
Phosphorus, 34
Photographic paper, 105
Pickles Warehouse, 94
Pig caster, 42
Pig iron, 22, 34-40, 41, 42, 43, 45, 46
Pike o'Stickle, 2
Pillar and stall, 25
Pirt, Joseph, 54-55
Pit wheel, 65
Pitch, 107
Pitstead, 89
Pittard, Mr, 56
Potash kiln, 94
Potash soap, 94, 100
Pratchitt's foundry, 54-55
Print works, 88
Printing (textiles), 103, 106
Pug mill, 34
Pulley, 30
Pylon, 5, 9
Quarry, 2, 3-7, 17
Quay, 118, 119
Quern, 61
Quick lime, 16
Rails, 40, 49-52, 114, 120
Railways, 29, 30, 31, 32, 34, 40, 52, 53, 54, 113, 114-116
Rainforth Hodgson, 83
Raised bog, 18
Ramsden, James, 120
Randall & Porter, 105
Ratten crook, 53
Ravenglass, 64, 116
Ravenglass & Eskdale Railway Preservation Society, 116
Ravenhill Pit, 15
Rawes Mill, 96-97
Rawlinson, William, 33
Reckitts, 110
Reel, 79, 81
Reservoir, 80, 105
Retting pond, 100
Rincing, 81

River Bela, 114-5
River Caldew, 106
River Cocker, 69, 88
River Derwent, 69, 119
River Gowan, 97
River Kent, 72, 104
River Lune, 88, 99, 113
Riving (slate), 3, 5,
Riving (wood), 77
Roads, 108, 111-114
Robinson's Brewery, 70
Rochester, 122
Roger Ridding, 94
Rogerson, Len, 36, 38, 39
Rolling mill, 40, 49-52, 75
Roman, 1, 3, 10, 16, 57, 113-114
Ropeway, 5, 8
Roughing, 81
Roughing mill, 40, 49-50
Rough-out, 2
Roughton Gill, 10-11
Rowan, 80
Royal Ordnance Factory, 67
RSPB, 32
Rubby Banks Mill, 100-101
Runner stone, 63, 65
Rusland, 22, 76, 86-88, 89, 94
Sailcloth, 103
Saltom Pit, 14-15
Sammel, 90, 91
Samuel Gawith & Co, 71
Sand, 22, 24, 25, 27, 34, 38, 42
Sandgate Farm, 93
Sandstone, 1, 65, 88
Sawmill, 54, 72, 88
Saying, saying barrel, 91, 92
Sayles, 75
Scafell Pike, 2
Scales, 16
Scotching, 100
Seaplane, 122
Seaves, 90, 91
Sedbergh, 12, 97, 99
Shaddon Mill, 105
Shaft (mining), 12, 15, 24, 25, 27-30
Shaft (tool), 80

Shafting (line), 80
Shap, 17
Shap granite, 63
Shearing, 93
Sheep, 93, 94, 111
Shipbuilding, 117, 120-121
Shoe making, 86, 102
Short Sunderland aircraft, 122
Sieve, 72, 73
Silloth, 65-66
Silver, 10, 11
Skelsmergh, 59, 79, 80
Slag, 21, 33, 34, 35-37, 41, 42-43
Slaked lime, 16
Slate, 3-7, 88, 117
Slate river, 5
Sledge, 3
Sludge remover, 107
Smelt mill, 11, 13
Snipey, 31
Snuff, 71-74, 88
Soaking pit, 40, 47, 49
Soap, 94, 100
Soapery Lane, 70
Sodium carbonate, 107
Solway, 18, 117, 120
Sourmilk Gill, 95
Spark Bridge bobbin mill, 79, 82
Spark Bridge cotton mill, 103
Specularite, 21
Speed limit, 117
Spells (spelks), 77
Sphagnum, 18
Spinning, 95, 96, 97. 102, 103, 105, 106
Spinning jenny, 96, 97
Spinning mule, 96, 97
SS Oriana, 120-121
Stagg, Joseph Dickinson, 14
Stagg condenser, 14
Stake Pass, 112
Stalker Bros, 53
Starter box, 59
State Management (breweries), 67-68
Staveley, 79, 81, 96, 97, 104

127

Steam engine (railway), 115, 116
Steam engine (stationary), 15, 22, 27, 28, 34, 49, 54, 66, 80, 97
Steam power, 54, 65, 66, 70, 79, 97, 100, 103, 105
Steam turbine, 28
Steel, 17, 23, 40, 53, 75
Steel Green, 24
Steel making, 17, 23, 40, 41, 45-48
Stockholm Tar, 85
Stocks Bobbin Mill, 59
Stone axe, 1, 2, 111
Stone crane, 65
Stone nuts, 65
Stony Hazel, 22-23
Stott Park, 80, 81, 82
Stramongate Mill, 99
Stringhearth, 21
Submarine, 117, 120
Sugar, 67, 118
Sulphur, 34, 107
Sulphur dioxide, 107
Swaledale sheep, 93, 98
Swallowmire, 75
Swill basket, 34, 77
Sycamore, 78, 80, 84
Tailrace, 95, 101
Tallow, 94
Tampimex Oil Products Ltd, 9
Tanner's beam, 88
Tannery, 86-88, 105
Tanning, 86-88.
Tapping (furnace), 35, 37, 38, 42
Tar, 44, 85
Tata Steel, 40
Taws, 77
Taylor, Richard, 76
Teazing, 98
Tebay, 113
Teeming, 41, 47, 48
Tenter ground, tenter hooks, 95
Tenterbank, 95
Terry Bank Tarn, 88
Textile mills, 58, 62, 94-106
Thompson, E.W., 99
Thrim, 85

Thursgill Mill, 58
Thwaites Mill, 62
Tipper trucks, 31
Tobacco, 71-74
Tom Rudd Beck, 88
Tool handles, 82
Top-slicing, 25
Tourism, 116, 117
Tow (textiles), 103
Troutbeck Bridge, 60, 81, 122
Tun (brewing), 67
Tun (milling), 63
Turbary, 18
Turbine – steam, 28
Turbine – water, 12, 34, 59-60, 80, 107
Turk (trade sign), 71
Turnpike roads, 111, 112-114
Tuyere, 34, 41, 45, 47
Tweed, 98, 105
Twine, 85, 103
Ullswater, 117
Ultramarine blue, 107
Ulverston, 23, 70, 77, 83, 104, 117
Underskiddaw, 97
Urine, 100
Vaux Breweries, 70
Vein (mineral), 1, 10, 11, 12, 21, 28
Via ferrata, 4
Viaduct, 114-115
Vickers & Co, 120, 122
Vielle Montagne Zinc Co, 14
Volcanic tuff, 2
Wad, 1
Walking beam furnace, 49
Walling, Cecil, 18
Walling, Larry, 18-19
Wallower, 65
Walney, 122
Warwick Bridge, 103, 105
Wasdale, 112
Water transport, 117-121
Water-lift, 34
Watermill, 57-59, 61, 62-65, 71-73, 80, 97
Waterwheel, 10, 22, 34, 57-59, 61, 65, 72, 80, 82, 88, 95, 97, 100, 103, 107

Waterwheel, mid-high breast, 58
Waterwheel, overshot, 59
Waterwheel, pitchback 59
Waterwheel, undershot 57, 72
Weaving, 77, 95, 96, 97, 99, 100, 102, 105, 106
Webster, Francis, 72
Weighbridge, 88
Wetherlam, 1
Wheel pit, 13, 14, 57, 95
While, Augustus, 33
While, Dennis, 33
While, J.M., 33
White Cross Bay, 122
White, Alan, 50
Whitebeck Mill, Burton, 61
Whitehaven, 1, 14-15, 23, 71, 78, 111, 118-119
Whitehaven Colliery Co, 119
Whitwell Mark & Co, 70
Wigton, 17, 61
Wilkinson, Isaac, 56
Williamson Bros, 60, 80
Wilmot, Mr, 77
Wilson, Cammel & Co, 41
Winder, Joseph, 54
Windermere, 87, 94, 115, 117, 122
Winding engine, 12, 15, 28
Windmill, 61
Witherslack, 18-20
Witherslack Corn Mill, 59
Woad, 94
Wood turning, 79-83
Woodland, 75-76
Wool, 93-99
Wool Growers Ltd, 93
Wool sack, 93-94
Woollen mill, 88, 97-99, 104, 105
Workington, 15, 23, 40-52, 54-55, 119-120
Wrought iron, 22, 23, 33, 40
Wythop, 95
Yeast, 67
Yo-yo, 79
Zinc, 1, 8-9, 14